EVOLVING BEAUTY

The Business of Beauty IN A NEW AGE

PHYLENCIA TAYLOR

Cover Illustration by SALAVSU. Book design by PRO360Design. Portions of this book were edited by Julie Sergel.

ISBN: 978-1530863990

First Printing, 2016. All Rights Reserved. Includes Index. Shine New Age Media is a division of Shine Exposition, LLC.
2451 Cumberland Parkway, Suite 3960, Atlanta, Ga 30339.

This book may be used for educational, business or sales promotional use, forward inquiries to the above address. v2.

FOR

Chance,
My Amazing Evolving Boy

DEDICATED TO

Dream Chasers, Freedom Followers, and Change Agents:

Those who believe in themselves enough to Try and Do.

ACKNOWLEDGMENTS

Throughout my ever-evolving journey,
many have contributed
blessings, lessons and sometimes both.
You know who you are.

Love + Light to My Tribe.
Chance T., Helen E., Tiffany A., Yvette B, Charese J.,
Kim B., Kya B., Kim R., Kim W., and Tracy D.

SHINE NEWAGEMEDIA

CONTENTS

FOREWORD

I started making beauty products in my kitchen over two decades ago. I started with moisturizers, wonderful "butters" and "milks" for the body because I had the driest skin in America. Then, I moved onto hair because at the time I always settled for what was available on the market for hair care. I was never truly happy and I discovered, quickly, that I wasn't the only one.

In 1993, my mother, Carol, encouraged me to sell my body butters and oils at a church flea market. With a $100 investment, my hobby was transformed into a business. Beauty influencers for Carol's Daughter were my family, friends, and friends of friends who happened to be celebrities. Halle Berry and Jada Pinkett-Smith talked about the brand because they loved it.

There wasn't a marketing budget for building relationships with people of influence. The Internet and social media weren't invented yet and people shopped over the phone and in person. The Carol's Daughter brand evolved organically, by word-of-mouth. My distribution outlets were craft fairs and flea markets. I had customers shopping out of my home for six years until I opened my first store in Fort Greene, Brooklyn. Carol's Daughter evolved from a home-based business into a multi-million-dollar empire through the support of celebrity investors, brand ambassadors, nine moniker stores and a variety of retail partnerships.

By 2013, due to underperformance and as part of our increased focus on retail channels, we decided to close five of our stores. Less than a year later, in November 2014, L'Oreal USA announced they were going to buy the brand — my brand, a brand I worked 21 years to create. A brand I named lovingly

1

after my mother, Carol. For that reason alone, Carol's Daughter will always carry a piece of me. I'm astonished and amazed at the progress this brand, my baby, has made. Many people thought that due to the sale, I would leave. Retire. Not so. This is what I do. It is who I am and it is my passion. I was not going to leave the brand behind. I still go into the office everyday and continue to play an integral role in the development process. After all, I want my great- great- grandchildren to walk into a store one day and still see what I built and made sitting on the shelves.

I share this background because it's a glimpse of the Carol's Daughter story, #BornandMade in Brooklyn. Our brand journey speaks to the same dynamics outlined in this book. Phylencia Taylor knows the business. I met her during the time between the multi-million-dollar investment stage of Carol's Daughter and our country's unfortunate economic decline. She was hired as Senior Marketing Manager in our Tribeca office to manage our hair care portfolio (restaging the Carol's Daughter Hair Milk brand and repositioning our Rosemary Mint shampoo and conditioner).

When I first met Phylencia I knew she was strong and smart and determined. I loved that she was an entrepreneur. She knew what hard work was and the rewards that come from that work. As I got to work with her more, especially during the business trips to HSN in Florida, I understood that no matter what path her career would take her, she would ride that road. If there was an obstacle, she would flow around it and her determination would not be shaken.

It makes so much sense that Phylencia would write this pivotal guide for the beauty industry. She wants it to thrive. She wants small businesses to mean big business—and she knows how to do it. She's a go-getter and an innovator. Grass does not grow under her feet unless she needs it for cushion to take her next steps.

Her knowledge, experience and expertise of the beauty industry are exceptional. The mind-blowing proprietary algorithm, A New Age Beauty Breakthrough Theorem™ truly sets her apart in the business of building beauty brands. I work with all of the industry people that this book was made to support, from brand managers, to bloggers to beauty professionals. I honor and endorse the rich resources contained within. *Evolving Beauty* articulates with understanding, the *evolving business of beauty*, an industry altered by social media, and the resounding transformation of the Multi-Cultural beauty space.

People and culture will forever change the beauty industry. Phylencia knows how to navigate and make smart brand decisions for small start-ups (like I was twenty years ago) and larger brands (like the one I've become).

This book is a game changer. A must-read for both Beauty Brand Executives and Beauty Influencers. The NEW AGE of BEAUTY is historic—and A New Age Breakthrough Theorem™ is a breakthrough tool for success in the ever-changing, always evolving, business of beauty.

Peace & Love,
Lisa Price
Founder of Carol's Daughter Born in Brooklyn,
Made with Love.

INTRODUCTION

"Don't sit down and wait for opportunities to come, get up and make them."
~Madame CJ Walker, Beauty Entrepreneur

The First U. S. Female Millionairess in the U.S. Guinness Book of World Records

Hello.

My name is Phylencia Taylor. I'm a Beauty Consultant and a Beauty Culturalist. My business is helping brands to build theirs (business) — from independent entrepreneurs to established Fortune 500 companies — utilizing a variety of marketing and communication tactics. As a Beauty Culturalist, studying the impact of the beauty industry on culture (women, identity, image, socialization, patterns, and purchase power) helps to understand how beauty shapes the world around us. It's a complex and layered subject.

It's ironic that I am writing a printed (and an E-Book) about the digital influence of the Beauty Industry, among other things, but my love of the industry and with so few *current* books about the Multi-Cultural beauty experience, I believe the time is *now*.

I've been in the beauty industry for 15 years, working with and for over 50 brands in the business. There's the formal education of a BBA from Clark Atlanta University and an MA from American University, but honestly, I've learned the most about marketing and communication throughout my career via on-the-job training. Worlds of knowledge were birthed in me while producing national campaigns like Bailey's Beauty Shop and Crown Royal's Barber Shop.

Experiences that taught me ridiculous amounts of wisdom and information included helping to build startup beauty brands like The Wonder Ker (a Luxury/Prestige Keratin Infused Satin Pillowcase) and The Honey Pot (a Specialty/Mass All Natural Feminine Wash). Also, by working with "the best in the business," from mid-range beauty sales magnate, GBL Sales, Inc. to large Fortune 500 brands like Carol's Daughter, Johnson Products and Wella Corporation of North America. Producing lifestyle national campaigns and special projects for mogul corporations such as PepsiCo, LVMH, Diageo, Sean John Enterprises and Stompin' on the Yard (a college tour later adapted as a feature film), helped to form perspectives and a macro understanding of the industry. A comprehensive view of beauty that academia in a more traditional sense, just couldn't do.

Working on micro and macro levels has offered both luxury and inconvenience. The advantage, a broadband of skills that spread across all marketing and beauty disciplines. There's benefit and bargain (labor) in working with an assortment of teams: finance, creative, account, research, manufacturing, production, marketing, and sales, seemingly simultaneously — and far too often. LOL. In short, I've made a lot of companies and independent entrepreneurs a lot of revenue and fancy profits through my expertise, management skills (people and projects), and understanding value and hard work.

As a former Corporate and Agency Executive, developing an innate understanding of the operational wants and needs required on both sides of the business, was another part of my education. From an Agency perspective, working in a function of Brand Service held an array of roles including Project Manager, Account Executive and VP of Client Services. My career in Marketing & Communication (MarComm) grew at U.S. Concepts, an experiential marketing agency known today under the MKTG moniker. Their core client was the largest purveyor of luxury wine and spirits on the market — LVMH and Diageo, which includes brands like Moët Hennessy, Moët & Chandon, Dom Perignon, Krug, Johnnie Walker, Tanqueray, Ruffino and Casa Lapostolle wines, amongst others.

Working with smaller agencies such as Vital Marketing, Cross-Walk Productions and Kinetix Integrated Communications, fostered additional business skills and helped me to appreciate the non-traditional, less orthodox approach, to getting the job done. It was a critical time for integrated learning while living in Manhattan. Smaller consulting, advertising, event and promotional agencies have business models similar to today's beauty start-ups.

As Campaign Producer, it was my responsibility to evolve something from nothing (another similarity to the current birthing role of beauty start-ups and Beauty Influencers). My charge was to maintain healthy and positive client relationships, to serve as the client's voice by providing the necessary brand foresight, and to deliver dynamic campaigns using clear objectives and success metrics. *More about measurement in future chapters.* Ultimately, I rallied the team to execute and liaise with the client from beginning to end.

From a Corporate perspective, there was so much room for growth within each role: from Sampler to Territory Account Manager, to Regional Account Executive and then, Senior National Director. My responsibilities helped solidify brand positioning with core objectives and managed deliverables for execution, with comprehensive reporting. New launch strategies required supportive price setting, forecasting, creative briefing, directing public relations, and managing the execution team (at that time there was no real digital presence). In collectively getting the job done, second only to effective communication, nothing has proven more valuable to a successful implementation than the ability to report successes and integrate industry metrics as confirmation. As Brand Manager, you become a corporate insider, an "inside-entrepreneur," or "Intrapreneur," as you're granted a certain level of autonomy. In this way, you take on the brand as if it were your own.

It's best to start with the budget and decide how to allocate funds. Budget and P&L (profit and loss statements) are key to a brand's success or failure, in any era. I've managed P&L's that exceeded $5 billion dollars. *More on budgeting in future chapters.*

The greatest success in leading cross-functional teams comes from clear communication and expectations. The speed and efficiency of the digital age is undeniable. It offers the ability to email, text or direct message (DM) information that you want communicated to a small or large group instantaneously. It's truly revolutionary and a core part of the New Age.

That said, it's equally important to cater to the need for direct human contact through human communication, even in a digital age, and especially amongst Baby Boomers (those born before 1963). Baby Boomers come from an era when technology wasn't as primary or prevalent. They're seasoned professionals (often senior managers; if lucky, mentors) who've worked hard, and come from a different time. They also tend to believe if you arrive early, you're a better employee than the employee that stays or comes in on weekends. For the most part, they are a bit less flexible in their thinking and operations.

The dismissal of human-to-human communication can be perceived as rude, disinterested or non-productive. In my experience, Generation Xers (those born between 1963 - 1980) are often split on the digital / face-to-face divide, based on their age. Generation Xers are often "the doers" and "the producers."

The babies of the groups, the Millennials (born between 1980 - 1995), often prefer limited to zero face-to-face communication. Unfortunately, many lack the experience or cognitive skills to eliminate the need for a physical demonstration or discussion about the project.

Lastly, regardless of age, it's always paramount to provide status updates to stakeholders. Over- communicating in the digital age is very necessary, where physical presence has limitations. Baby Boomers seek more physical contact and Millennials seek less.

Understanding the importance of communication while deciding to remain in corporate America, (and being two- thirds of the way into my career, well into my 30s), I decided to go back to school—graduate school. I leveraged the corporate marketing experience gained in NYC and returned to Washington, DC, to complete a Master's degree in Strategic Communication. I quickly discovered the campaigns I'd been developing for years were successful because they were fully integrated, 360 degree campaigns. They touched the consumer where they lived, and were based upon cultural ideologies and patterns.

Exposure to both sides of the business (Agency and Corporate) has afforded me vital first-hand experience where I've been able to learn the beauty industry and create brand growth simultaneously. The agencies helped me to evolve with a cognitive understanding of business practices that transcend disciplines and industries. This was invaluable— and really set me apart. Working in wine and spirits at U.S. Concepts as a Promotional Assistant (a fancy name for a Sampler) is where I grew to understand the layers involved with developing marketing and communication campaigns. Back in those days (the mid-to-late 1990s), a Sampler was a young (attractive) woman who distributed complimentary drink cards as a method of consumer trial, with the goal of consumer purchase or conversion in bars or clubs. I started in 1996 as a Promotional Assistant working in Washington, DC, and resigned in 2001, as Senior National Account Director working in New York City. I saw firsthand—from the bottom up—the direct impact of campaigns on every level. This advantage gave me a keen perspective for development, execution, and analysis—all 360 degrees of it.

It was during this time at U.S. Concepts that I began to understand social culture and psychographic archetypes in the wine and spirit consumer. The drinking culture where a certain aged consumer goes out to drink a certain type of aged spirit, in a specific glass, with or without a particular mixer, neat or on the rocks, poured by a (usually) gorgeous and familiar bartender or mixologist, starting at a precise time of day or evening, driven in a specific type of car, wearing certain clothing, going to a distinct category of bar, lounge, club or super club—consumed at a strategic price point.

And then there's Bottle Service. Sure, it existed back then, but nothing like today's "Exclusive VIP Bottle Parade Procession" complete with a DJ mix, light show and fireworks. It was during this time, as Senior Account Executive at U.S. Concepts with Moët Hennessy, where I helped create, develop, manage and analyze 15 Key Demographic Market Areas (DMAs), with over 500 event promotions a year. I traveled to Épernay and the Cognac regions of France with corporate teams to understand growth, crush (harvest time), the production process— essentially how these billion dollar businesses started. I gained an intrinsic understanding of the wine and spirits culture, it's subcultures, and later on, unbeknownst to me, figured out how it all translated to beauty.

ARE WE TALKING BEAUTY AND CULTURE?

Culture is "a set of customary beliefs, social forms, and material traits of a racial, religious, or social group. Culture is the behavior, beliefs and characteristics of a particular social, ethnic, or age group: A set of shared attitudes, values, goals and practices that characterize a behavior, belief, value and symbol that they accept, generally without thinking about them, and passed along by communication and imitation from one generation to the next." (Merriam-Webster Dictionary, 2016)

Many U.S. brands market culture as represented by a specific ethnic group. Yet, to classify the drinking culture or the beauty culture, today it speaks more to the consumer's utility for the product or sensibilities surrounding it, to a specific interest. With today's evolving population schemas, ethnicity now has nearly nothing to do with a product's consumption culture.

Today, culture is defined as having a *cultural sensibility* related more to lifestyle. And so, "Urban" no longer means predominately African American and "Suburban" no longer means just General Market, segmented in marketing as the Caucasian masses. Old cultural definitions, labels and categories are passé. Urban, suburban and rural consumers across the country buy beauty products. In beauty, the distinction is by product utility for hair, body and skin. The future of beauty products will center around consumer product wants and needs as it relates to hair texture, skin color and melanin composition.

Understanding the wine and spirits connection with culture, subculture, and product consumption, offered a deeper perspective and enlightened connection with my true love, the Beauty Industry. Pursuing a career in the Beauty Industry has been a constant. I've always gravitated back to it, in between agency position escapades. The impact of beauty—how brands transcend culture, how beauty shapes a woman's image, identity, and the world—is forever inspiring.

For most women, the expression of beauty is directly related to her self-esteem, financial status and her ability to evolve socially. I'm anti those social norms. I totally support the individual pursuit of beauty for women—free of outside factors. In fact, The Natural Hair Movement "beautifully" resolves this pursuit. *More about the natural movement and culture in coming chapters.*

ENTREPRENEURIAL INSPIRATION

In 2007, I started Shine Exposition, LLC, a Beauty Trade Show in partnership with the Indiana Black Expo. Shine Exposition was conceived with three others: Nicole Robinson (today an Art Exhibition & Campaign Producer), and her "partner" both from New Orleans, and the late Madinah Grier, a New Jersey resident (former Marketing Executive, may she Rest In Power). It was Nicole who thought of the name Shine. I met her at Cross-Walk, and met Madinah at Wella Corp.

In less than a year we all morphed into our own direction. I continued Shine Exposition and transferred the operations independently. Based on my love for and my experience within the industry, it was natural to begin to offer Beauty Business Consultation. My interest in the culture and socialization of beauty remained, while the business evolved to create Shine Magazine—a quarterly print magazine for Beauty Professionals and Enthusiasts. The magazine delivered Beauty Professional Industry News and included series like: "The Rise of the Dominican Salon," "Why Are There So Few Ethnic Beauty Distributors vs. So Many Ethnic Beauty Consumers?" and "The Black Barbershop's Country Club Culture."

With the collapse of the print industry, Shine Magazine evolved yet again, as Shine Beauty Culture (SBC), the Research and Brand Management Consultancy we are today. SBC is the power behind *Evolving Beauty*, The Business of Beauty in A New Age, which includes: the blog, EvolvingBeauty.info; this book, an atlas for navigation in the Beauty Industry today, and a forthcoming educational and cultural communication resource, and series in the beauty business.

WHY DID I WRITE THIS BOOK?

As much as I love digital and social media, I love the business of beauty, and the artistry of marketing and communication even more. I love helping others build their brands and navigate in this New Age of Beauty. Working in the industry, I see so many enthusiastic indie brands rise onto the scene with such promise, and yet make so many costly mistakes because of their inexperience or inability to navigate within the industry. At the heart of this book is *modern day beauty marketing layered with digital influence — to breed success*.

I wrote this book to share tactics that work — tactics I've learned and adapted over the last 15 years in business to help build, maintain and prosper brands. My passion is the Beauty Industry and I know how to guide indie brands from their starting place, wherever that is. I've assisted established brands in staying relevant and increasing market share through modern tactics and innovation. I've managed beauty bloggers to create added value for their brand clients while expanding their value and business with greater ease and understanding. I want businesses to create legacies, to know long lasting results and obtain solid monetization. My ultimate goal in working with beauty brands is to increase revenue and market share while yielding larger profit margins.

The heart and ambition of this book is to share the 15 years of brand building experience within the Beauty Industry. But an equally important force is the importance of diversity and inclusion in beauty. Inclusion is not an option. It's a requirement. And the time is now to embrace the impending Multi-Cultural population explosion.

Already, Multi-Cultural, or ethnic minorities, have grown

from 10 percent in 1950, to 30 percent of the population in 2015. Today, minorities are majorities in 50 U.S. cities. In 10 U.S. states, the Caucasian population is the minority. By 2040, 50 percent of the U.S. will be Multi-Cultural or made up of what was, the ethnic minority. And so, traditional labels in culture will shift. Half Black, half Mexican, known as "Blaxicans," as well as half Mexican, half Filipina, known as "Mexipinos," are helping to redefine the culture in the U.S. *(US Census, 2015, Atlanta Tribune Magazine, 9/2015)*

> *"The beauty of the world lies in the diversity of its people [and Culture]"* ~**Unknown**

NEGOTIATED BEAUTY

Hair is one of the most, if not *the* most important dynamic of a woman's beauty, particularly for women of color. "Our hair is our glory," as reiterated in the book *Queens*, by Cunningham and Alexander. The majority of women of color have textured hair. That is, hair that has variation, measure or the disposition of hair defined by shape, size and density. Hair is either straight, wavy, curly or kinky/coily. All hair, everyone's hair on the planet, can be defined in one of these categories. For a more detailed examination of hair, find your type using Oprah Winfrey's long time hairstylist, Andre Walker's hair chart. His book, *Hair Talks*, released in 1997, offers The Andre Walker Hair Type Classification System, which helps define your hair category from a 1 (straight) to 4C (kinky/coily). Textured hair products are categorized by section in the Beauty Industry as the "Multi-Cultural Hair Care Section."

For centuries, and still debatable today, if a woman does not have straight hair, isn't beyond a certain skin color, or does not align with global or societal beauty standards, then she is forced to negotiate her beauty and change her looks. Meaning a woman is forced to negotiate her beauty — to compromise her hair style, even at the expense of her health (from exposure and the application of chemical treatments) and often, even her identity. What is the goal in all of this transformation? Social acceptance, social classification, upward mobility and financial gain.

The 1960s and 70s birthed the "I'm Black and I'm Proud" Black Power movement, which developed legendary brands and companies that spoke to an energetic, proud and rebellious African American consumer. Natural hair and afros were worn freely. Nonconformity was met collectively with an independent spirit. Pioneers joined trailblazers and a new era in The Black Haircare Industry was born. Two great forefathers of the ethnic haircare revolution of the 20th Century include the Luster and Johnson families. In 1957, Fred Luster Sr. founded Luster Products. In 2016 it's still a family owned business, the oldest family owned ethnic haircare business in the U.S. In 1954, George Johnson Sr. launched Johnson Products Company with Ultra Wave Hair Culture, a "permanent" hair straightener for men that can be applied at home. Women's chemical straighteners followed. Today Johnson Products is owned by St. Cloud Capital LLC, an investment company, managed by Dr. Miracles.

WOMEN BUILT THE BEAUTY INDUSTRY

The Beauty Industry was built by women from modest and meek backgrounds. They were door-to-door sales women who grew their empires during a period of changing social attitudes on beauty and women's roles. These women lived in a time when social pursuit of the beauty industry and enterprising was considered immoral. They were forced to create new forms of direct sales (pyramid type of organization) and marketing tactics. Today's distribution methods were unavailable. The women who built the beauty industry were innovators, they created the once non-existent consumer market for beauty products by combining products and services in salons, creating a culture of social events and through job creation for women — who were also the consumers of these products.

Think about the trailblazing women of the Beauty Industry in the 1920's. Annie Malone has been credited for inventing the hot comb. Madame CJ Walker created "The Wonderful Hair Grower," a scalp conditioning and healing formula product line with a revolutionary door-to-door sales strategy. Both women created enterprises, making them the first female millionaires in the United States, (Latson, 2014) though Madame CJ Walker is credited by this wealth in the Guinness Book of World Record.

In 1910, Walker was featured in the Guinness Book of World Records as the first American female self-made millionaire. (Guinness Book of World Records, 1919) Walker popularized the Press-and-Curl style. Today the style would result in what is known as a "Silk Press" with a flat iron, versus a "Press-and-Curl" style with a straightening comb.

By the 1960s and 70s, iconic brands like Afro Sheen, Ultra Sheen, TCB, Bronner Brothers and Luster's Pink Oil, had become household names. This was largely due to the rise in the "I'm Black and I'm Proud" Movement. In the 1980s, these companies introduced chemical relaxers. This was, in short, a response to women seeking acceptance in the workplace for financial empowerment, quite simply to take care of their families — and for upward mobility.

The void in the marketplace of ethnic brands and collective brand efforts prompted the formation of the American Health & Beauty Aids Institute (AHBAI), founded in 1981. AHBAI, a national trade association represents the world's leading companies which produce haircare, skincare and shaving products for the ethnic consumer. AHBAI is branded by the

Proud Lady Symbol and supports community investment within communities by providing jobs and scholarships. Again, and to emphasize the point, the need for inclusion is evident by organizations like AHBAI and defenders of inclusion within the Beauty Industry.

Bethann Hardison, fashion activist and former model, has been championing diversity in fashion for decades. In a September 2015 WWD article, Hardison said "The more designers who use people of color, any color, not just African-Americans, the better." Iman, supermodel and owner of Iman Cosmetics, has been a long-time supporter of Hardison.

Models around the world are both stunned and grateful for the bravery of supermodel Nykhor Paul, who gives voice to the reality of racism in the fashion industry. She's boldly addressed the lack of make-up artists (MUA) astute in color complexion hues. MUA provide a service in the beauty industry for a variety of models of all backgrounds. Women of color included. The ability to match skin color—especially in regards to matching makeup to skin tone, should be a given. She calls them out for not pushing themselves to do the research to ensure every model on the runway looks their best. "Just because you only book a few of us," said Paul, "doesn't mean you have the right to make us look ratchet. I'm tired of complaining about not getting booked as a black model and I'm definitely tired of apologizing for my blackness."

Nykhor Paul's sentiments of the industry are not uncommon. Her experience rings true for so many in the fashion industry. Yet diversity in beauty transcends beauty categories, like packaged goods or runway fashion. Diversity is a global concern.

For many years, Luster's was the only major African-American owned beauty company that remained from the independent mogul heydays of the 70s and 80s. But today there's a resurgence of African-American owned beauty businesses, primarily due to *The 21st Century Natural Hair Movement.* One critical distinction in the *new naturals movement* — different from the1970s — is that economic empowerment is not a sacrifice for a woman's freedom of expression. Wearing hair natural, free from chemical relaxers, ushers a newfound confidence that demands acceptance, rather than passively requesting it through hair relaxed.

Today, Black-owned haircare brands like Shea Moisture, Alikay Naturals, Mielle Organics, Miss Jessie's and Mixed Chicks deliver a powerful presence with on shelf and e-commerce sales, contributed because of the new *Naturals Movement,* coupled with the Digital Age.

And so, this book was written to inform small and big brands in A New Age of Beauty so that Beauty Executives and Influencers are better prepared for success, with proven insider tactics my experience. And, to create another space and another voice for the advocacy of diversity and inclusion in beauty. I hope to instigate and inspire the power of beauty in our business.

Each chapter of this book outlines sound tactics for modern keep beauty marketing and communication that reference skin, color cosmetics, body and haircare. African American, or Black hair care, is a reoccurring focus throughout the book. Primarily because of the robust sales and image concerns for women of color. African American haircare, or Multi-Cultural haircare, also lead the path at retail, for diversity in beauty.

BRAND EXECS + BEAUTY INFLUENCERS = SUCCESS

There's a powerful force that offers a unique and critical mass of brand awareness and ultimately, sales, when right partnerships are forged between brand and brand influencers. It's unfortunate when beauty brand executives continue to hire bloggers, vloggers, and other celebrity influencers, with little to no impact or results, delivering disjointed campaigns all while wasting money and time.

When beauty brands (both new indie start-ups and established brands) aren't internally secure with solid foundational tactics (like those outlined in the chapters of this book), they're setting themselves up for failure and loss of revenue. Beauty brands should have unwavering mastery foundation that include strong positioning, point of difference and overall focus. Beauty Influencers must partner with brands that resonate with their businesses.

Successful campaigns can be built with confidence by influencer and blogger brands who have a clear *brand essence*, solid *culturally cued research* analysis, a *niche audience*, are cognizant of *comprehensive competitive placement* (by price and position) and possess a strong *integrated marketing and communication* plan with success metrics. All of which are necessary for launching a new product or refreshing an existing one, with a fully-integrated marketing and communication campaign.

Without these elements, campaigns remain flat in consumer awareness and sales; essentially smoke and mirrors. And when the air clears and budgets are spent, brands will start the popular Beauty Influencer partnership all over again with a different influencer, and garner the same empty results. Brand Executives are left wondering why there wasn't greater awareness — and stronger sales — while Beauty

Influencers scurry to the next brand that offers a budget and a dream. Neither action speaks to brand integrity or effective long-term partnerships for consumer awareness, increased sales or a spirit of Brand Mastery. Let's put an end to Beauty Influencer promiscuity. Brand executives and Beauty Influencers can select the right partners who align with their respective brand equity and monetization goals.

WHAT YOU'LL LEARN FROM *EVOLVING BEAUTY*

Evolving Beauty is an atlas of proven tactics and practices to help stop financial bleeding. In it, you'll learn how to establish solid anchors, standards and expectations for your brand. You'll learn the minor and major business model adjustments you can make to help widen the door to greater presence and opportunity. *Evolving Beauty* reveals essential insider tactics gained from working with over 50 brands in the beauty industry, over a decade of experience as a Beauty Product Manager and Agency Executive. These successful tactics have been used on both sides of the business across multi-level, complex campaigns.

Each chapter is designed with proven marketing principles, layered with modern strategy and advantage, to assist and support Intreprenuers--Inside Corporate Brand Executives and Entrepreneurs—Start-Up Manufacturers, Product Brands and Beauty Influencers, Service Brands to build brands independently and unite collectively.

This book is designed so that you can start implementing strategies immediately. Enjoy a coherent and monetizing path to success in A New Age of Beauty. In the following pages, I'll lead you through real-life beauty practices that allow you to foster deeper, long-term relationships with serious monetizing potential. I'll show you how to adapt basic, yet modern marketing and communication principles, and apply them to today's rapid speed digital beauty business landscape for a larger audience, a stronger presence with long term returns.

Evolving Beauty initiates tactics that allow transparency in blockages to your business flow. You'll grasp how to build or re-build your brand from the ground up. It's so important to know YOU CAN develop and cultivate relationships in the business of beauty that you may have thought were beyond your grasp.

I don't think you've picked up this book by mistake. Maybe

it chose you? You have a yearning to stay relevant in the Beauty Industry and evolve alongside A New Age of Beauty. Whether you're an established owner wishing to refresh your brand with greater positioning? Or a Beauty Influencer (blogger, vlogger, celebrity status socialite, beauty brand ambassador) hoping to create a more potent presence, you'll learn what you need most, to evolve in the business of beauty.

You'll learn more about A NEW AGE OF BEAUTY. A triad of robust dynamics and challenging decisions required to help build beauty brands. THE BEAUTY BREAKTHROUGH THEROEM ™

A proprietary algorithm used as a navigation tool, created by Shine Beauty Culture Consultancy and I.

These three dynamics, when analyzed collectively, create a powerful brand building navigation tool for success.

1. Instant *Digital* outreach and response,
2. The *Multi-Cultural* *population explosion*
   - *Diverse consumer beauty product wants and needs.*
3. A *Brand Matrix* *of time, consumer choices and product cycles.*

Evolving Beauty, an atlas for integrated, synergized modern marketing and communication strategies. It will help you move forward when working with new or restaged product launches and campaigns. Most importantly, *Evolving Beauty* is an atlas of intersecting byways, in the ever evolving, business of beauty.

PART I

SET IT UP FOR SUCCESS IN A NEW AGE

1 THE BUSINESS OF BEAUTY IN A NEW AGE

"The beauty of the world lies in the diversity of it's people."
~Unknown.

The Business of Beauty in A NEW AGE is an era in history, beauty history, that has *never* existed before. Robust dynamics and challenging decisions are shaping the way beauty brands are being built. The 21st Century New Naturals Hair and Lifestyle Movement, coupled with instantaneous communication of the digital world, have forever transformed the Multi-Cultural beauty space. This movement, inspired in the U.S. in the early 2000's, created a global ripple and cultural paradigm shifting in beauty and identity norms. Women have opted to wear their hair chemically free from relaxers, and not straighten it, to instead embrace their natural curly/coily textures. For women with textured hair — hair is an extension of her identity.

This *New Naturals Hair Movement* pushes the envelope on healthy hair and acceptable hairstyles — creating community bonding, through hairstyles and beauty trade secrets. It further explores the critical cultural work that surrounds beauty standards. As the U.S. and the world become more Multi-Cultural and Multi-Racial, new beauty standards are in demand; Benchmarks of beauty evolve and are based upon blends of hair textures, with skin and bodies rich in a variety of hues.

BEAUTY — ILLUMINATED BY DIGITAL

Not only does A NEW AGE OF BEAUTY change the way brands are built, but it also transforms people and culture by the way in which we see ourselves in the world, the way we communicate, the methods we choose to socialize within, and the illumination of it all on digital and social media platforms. In this new way, the world engages, embraces, explores, learns and grows.

Through years of experience working with brands (from small indie brands to large Fortune 500 corporations) and understanding the price of costly mistakes, Shine Beauty Culture Consultancy has uncovered a triad of dynamics that have NEVER existed until this very time in history. These three dynamics, when analyzed collectively, create a powerful brand building navigation tool for imminent success. THE BEAUTY BREAKTHROUGH THEOREM™

Beauty brands require specific metrics of measure to make effective decisions. So whether you're a small start-up or a large, established brand, it's imperative to put the right navigational tools in place. THE BEAUTY BREAKTHROUGH THEOREM™ is just that—a proprietary algorithm used like a compass to guide successful brand decision making.

A theorem is a general proposition, not self-evident, but proven by a chain of reasoning. Whereas a theory is an idea confirmed by observation or experiment, according to the Shorter Oxford English Dictionary. A triad of factors, coupled with collectively analyzed robust marketplace dynamics, provides an evolutionary decision-making tool like never before:

THE BEAUTY BREAKTHROUGH THEOREM ™

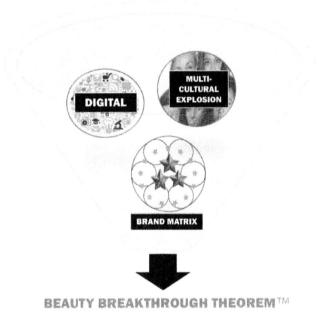

BEAUTY BREAKTHROUGH THEOREM™

A Navigation Tool--for Small Brands & Big Brands, Each Require a Different Measure.

NEW AGE OF BEAUTY

Source: Shine Beauty Culture Consultancy,

I. DIGITAL - Instant digital 2-way communication through social media platforms. Digital offers instantaneous consumer reach and response. A continuous measure of types of inbound or outbound communication is used and what do the analytics say about what's driving brand traffic and influencing sales, or a lack thereof?

II. MULTI-CULTURAL - The Multi-Cultural population explosion. By 2040, the minority population will become the majority population. *(U.S. Census, 2014)* African American, Hispanic, Asian and persons of Mixed Race will comprise over 50% of the U.S. population. The mixture of ethnicities will breed a fusion of hair textures and varied compositions of melanin in the skin. This assortment of hair grains and skin hues will require a new assortment of beauty products for specific consumer hair, body and skin needs.

III. BRAND MATRIX

> The Brand Matrix = Time + Consumer Choices + Product Cycles and Stages

Brand Matrix is the component that includes our proprietary algorithm, THE BEAUTY BREAKTHROUGH THEOREM ™. A *theorem* is an expression (or portion) of a general principle that makes it part of a larger concept to be recognized time and time again. And so, a tactic to determine where you are as a brand and to support brand decision making, is to use previously established marketing concepts and integrate them with a modern NEW AGE tool to set your course. By utilizing and integrating reasonable brand knowledge (information you already know), you can make tactical, rational decisions to set up your brand for success. *Let me explain quite simply how this works.*

The three stars in the Brand Matrix Diagram represent the following

> Product Life Cycle Theory (Vernon, 1966)
> Diffusion of Innovation Theory (Rogers, 1995)
> Brand Matrix (Taylor, 2016) Our modern approach to decision making navigation - THE BEAUTY BREAKTHROUGH THEOREM ™ (Taylor, 2016 — Shine Beauty Culture Consultancy)

★ *Product Life Cycle* - Vernon's Product Life Cycle concept (1966). This includes a sequence of stages that a new product progresses through and is associated with; Changes in the marketing situation, thus impacting marketing strategy and mix. *The stages include introduction, growth, maturity and decline.* Projection of revenue and profits are plotted on the chart throughout the stages.

In the *Introduction* stage, a brand seeks to build product awareness and develop a market for the product. In *Growth*, the brand seeks to build a consumer brand preference and increase market share. In *Maturity*, the brand must defend market share while maximizing profit. And in the *Decline* stage, the brand must add new features while maximizing profits.

★*Diffusion of Innovation Theory* - Founded by Everett M. Rogers (1962), a social scientist. The theory makes a distinction between five adopter categories classified on the basis of consumer speed of new product adoption as follows, from a to e until the market is saturated:

(a) Innovators - Risk takers, the first to try, easily adoptable to a new product.
(b) Early Adopters - Leaders, change easily and like new ideas; great tactics via how-to videos, informationals; they don't need information to adopt.
(c) Early Majority - Not known as leaders, but fairly quickly; stories and evidence convert early majority.
(d) Late Majority - Skeptics of change, only adopt after others have adopted (the majority); stories on how many likes. Followers and adopters appeal to the late majority.
(e) Laggards - Resisters, hardest group to convert; tied to tradition, very conservative. Pressure from other groups appeals to this group, including statistics, and fear tactics.

The Diffusion of Innovation Theory explains and predicts how people will adopt an idea or product. There are five stages that are involved with this theory:

1. Awareness/Knowledge — Mass media, advertising, application
2. Interest/Persuasion — Wanting more by seeking out further information such as website or blog
3. Trial/Decision — Try an idea, weigh pros and cons
4. Evaluation/Implementation — Interpersonal information
5. Adoption: Adopting new technology, making the change made

Essentially the Rate of Product Adoption. The four components of consumer choice as it relates to adoption of a new product include:

1. Innovation — the introduction of a new product or category.
2. Communication — how product awareness happens: word-of mouth, mass media, NEW AGE relevance (website and social media).
3. Time — how long it takes for a consumer to adopt or reject a product.
4. Social System (cultural dynamics) — the assessment of social norms as it relates to social behaviors and social influencers; understanding how information is spread within social systems is the foundation of understanding who your audience is and their sub- cultures are.

★*Brand Matrix* - Brand Matrix is a potent integration separate from the Product Life Cycle concept and the Diffusion of Innovation Theory. It provides pivotal foundational advancement for strategic marketing, coupled with a versatile navigation tool with distinction amongst small independent and larger established brands.

Limitations

- ➢ Product Life Cycle doesn't specify the amount of time a product may remain in a certain stage, or that each stage may be of varied times. It also suggests that some products die. Brands like Pond's face cream and Luster Products have been in existence for over 50 years. The Life Cycle theory can prompt unnecessary new product releases and cannibalize mature brands that may still have life. The theory supports small, independent brands, but not large ones. Lastly, it also doesn't support a restage or re-launch, as such tactics weren't often used when the theory was released in the 1960s.

- ➢ The Diffusion of Innovation Theory works well in beauty; as *behavioral product usage* is a great component to measure success. However, the influence of the digital age and social media influencers have escalated the adopter and majority stage adoption rates. Even so, the Diffusion of Innovation theory and adoption stages remain relevant in the digital age, A NEW AGE OF BEAUTY, with cognitive thinking about the brands stage. And so, here is where THE BEAUTY BREAKTHROUGH THEOREM ™ integrates nicely as a decision making tool in research, partnership and marketing mix support, to name a few MarComm components.

WHY THIS TOOL?

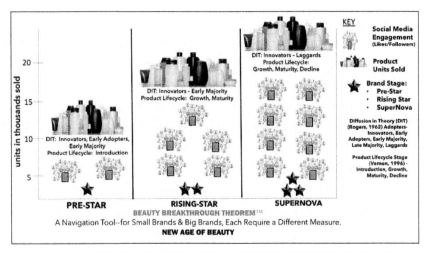

BRAND MATRIX-BEAUTYBREAKTHROUGH THEOREM™ -
Figure 1 – Design by Shine Beauty Culture Consultancy

Brand Matrix uses three beauty brand characteristics to assess the development of brand stages to help determine the next course of action.

> ➤ *Pre-Star -* ★- This Brand is on the verge of launching, with limited product units (less than 15,000). The brand needs buzz, awareness, sales, smart marketing and an effective course to build the brand. Sales tend to be primarily generated online and at trade shows. The bulk of time is spent testing brand perception with consumers and changing brand elements to retest. The brand is discovering who their star or hero product(s) are.

> ➤ *Rising-Star-* ★★ - This Brand has made headway with consumer relevance, notable sales and units produced. The brand has created some level of success: social media relevance, 2-way communication with consumers, online/e-commerce distribution and perhaps smaller

(limited) retail distribution. The Brand is retail ready, aimed for larger distribution. Star or hero product(s) have been identified.

> *SuperNova* ★★★ - This Brand is well known, U.S. distribution in play, and possibly International distribution. Maintaining market share with brand priority of continued growth. Brand has a robust social media presence and consumer recall. Marketing plan for the year includes testing or promoting new line extension(s). Star or hero products have reached maturity and may need a restage or line extension(s).

In short, our proprietary algorithm studies the specifics of the brand audience (social media audience reception), brand stage and life cycle. This data is analyzed to determine where the brand is in the Brand Matrix. A campaign's objectives should be made to reach a new brand stage, while courting consumers and raising trial/awareness and ultimately increasing sales and market share.

I. Instant Digital & Social Media Communication.
Direct dialogue between a brand, a consumer, and sometimes a Brand Influencer. It is instantaneous, accelerated digital consumer reach and response, at the speed of light. The digital age is time sensitive, an ever-evolving technology landscape with innovation moving at a high-speed. For instance, the speed of television and recording devices has facilitated a ripple of product releases in the marketplace over the last 15 years.

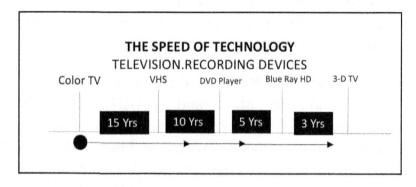

Source: Historyoftv.tv – Figure Design by: Shine Beauty Culture Consultancy

Social media has given a voice to the voiceless — exposure and connection to brands through authentic, underground inspiration, movement, and feelings — like never before. It offers instant sharing in similar or distinct communities that hasn't been afforded prior to this era in history. Perhaps the most powerful tool that digital and social media platforms supply is that of measurement of campaigns. The digital era grants exciting new metrics to measure the success or failure of a campaign (Google Analytics and other analytical data based tools), *which we'll discuss in future chapters.*

II. Cross-Cultural Product Explosion.

Diversification of products, along with wants and needs of the Cross-Cultural beauty product community and the new Cross-Cultural populations, are all essential to take note of. The explosion of Cross-Cultural, Multi-Cultural populations is transforming "face" of the population, are all supporting new consumer dynamics. New demands are and will be placed upon Research & Development for product innovation. Our global society is comprised of many hair textures: straight, wavy, curly, kinky, fine, coarse, or a combination of any of these. Significant because we're speaking about hair texture, not ethnicity. Also, new combinations of skin compositions are emerging, affecting make-up and skincare needs and wants. The amount of melanin in the skin influences sun and wrinkle damage, which directly affects product requirements relating to aging and overall beauty health.

> *By the year 2040, the ethnic majority will become the ethnic minority. Hispanics (28%), African Americans (17%) and Asians (8%) will comprise 53% of the U.S. Population. This percentage does not include Mixed Race, Native American or other people of color. (U.S. Census, 2012 and Population Estimates, 2014)*

With the African American (Black) population increasing to nearly 75 million by 2050, Multi-Cultural implications continue to influence the Beauty Industry. African Americans over-index in purchases compared to their General Market counterparts — purchasing nine times more, according to a 2015 Nielsen report. A new trend growing amongst the African American consumer is the Caribbean Influence: One out of every eleven African Americans is a Caribbean immigrant and one in every six African Americans will be an immigrant, by 2060. This enriches the cultural mix of U.S. Blacks and contributes to an overall rise in consumer education, affluence and purchasing power. Also, the African American youth and digital age relevancy is critically important to the NEW AGE OF BEAUTY. The average age of African Americans is younger, averaging 31.4 years, compared to 39 years, for the non- Hispanic, Caucasian population, or 36.7 years, for the total population *(Nielsen, 2015 Diversity Report).*

With focus upon natural hair offerings, growth factors definitely include the rising Multi-Cultural population, the Specific needs per ethnicity, increasing distribution/marketing, expansion of product offerings and intensified competition. [xii] These unique needs create an upswing in demand.

Beauty manufacturers are breaking boundaries between General Market and Multi-Cultural beauty with brands like Carol's Daughter and Shea Moisture. Mainstream brands like Maybelline, CoverGirl and Revlon, are also entering the Multi-Cultural personal care markets in haircare and make-up.

NEW AGE BEAUTY, NEW AGE BRANDS

Today's "BRAND" of beauty is being redefined. Bloggers are influencers but they're also brands. A great example of this is Afrobella. Founder of Afrobella.com, the "God-Mother of Brown Beauty Blogging," As she is affectionately known in the beauty industry. She has a beauty brand (not a product, but a service brand) where people and lifestyle enthusiasts go to for trusted information. She's an established journalist, beauty editor, blogger, and influencer and known speaker. Afrobella is the equivalent of a BRAND. A *Supernova* BEAUTY BRAND.

This is VERY SIGNIFICANT for the NEW AGE Blogger to comprehend—not only the sovereignty of it—but the application. Bloggers are BRANDS and should apply all dynamics of this book from that perspective.

In December 2015, Advertising Age released "The 7 Highest Paid Beauty Bloggers." Topping the list was Yuya (@lady16makeup), a Blogger who makes $41,000 a month. That's on YouTube alone, with over 12 million channel subscribers. Bottom line, Bloggers and Vloggers are a service beauty brand in and of themselves.

Beauty Influencers are the new kids in town. Celebrity socialites have long been used as brand ambassadors, but the dynamics of the digital and social media age have raised the bar. The industry as a whole is comprised of;

> ➤ **Beauty Brand Manufacturer** – Brand Executives, Corporate teams.

> **Beauty Influencers**-Beauty Bloggers, Vloggers, Celebrity Socialites/Ambassadors
> **The Audience** -the Consumer, the Target Market, the Prized followers.

The consumer of beauty is an ever-evolving product seeker, in perpetual pursuit of beauty.

THE FIRST BLOGGER

A student named Justin Hall is credited as being the first official Blogger. In 1994, he termed the website, links.net, his "personal home page." But it was the year 2005 that changed the world of social media forever. That year the term "web log" matured to "blog," a reported 32 million Americans were reading blogs, and an estimated $100 million worth of blog ads were sold, as reported by Huffington Post. A significant new career field was forged. Vlogging (by Vloggers) launched a new industry with video-created reports offering tips and first hand reviews on the usage of products with the introduction of YouTube in 2005.

The idea that Beauty Vloggers and Bloggers (non- Beauty Professionals) have monetized their efforts for lucrative careers, with tens and hundreds of thousands of followers — based upon their suggestions and opinions — it has raised a new bar in industry standards. It speaks volumes as to just how real the quest for the "right" products and practices are. Voids in the marketplace continually prompt African American Beauty Enthusiasts to use their ingenuity to leverage beauty products, unique product combinations and usage practices into their own hands.

Bloggers and Vloggers offer a modern reach to a precise demographic audience by talking directly about specific beauty products and services. If a brand partners with the "right" Blogger, it can increase brand awareness within their communities and influence consumer purchase decisions exponentially. The "right" Blogger is one who has an interest and benefit to the product and the campaign—is equally as appealing to their blog and target audience. Some Bloggers have diversified audiences, segmented by subcultural behavior. For example "Naturalistas," "Transitioners," and "Big Choppers," all represent natural hair and a healthy lifestyle. This segmentation creates a successful targeted approach for the campaign and the Blogger. For a campaign to be successful, the Blogger, Brand and the audience must have a strong mutual interest and be completely invested.

The Beauty Industry will reach an estimated **$81 billion by 2017** *(EuroMonitor International, 2015)*. The segment of the population known as Multi-Cultural (Ethnic, Black, African American) lead with product class sales in Haircare, followed by Make-up (color cosmetics), and then Skin & Body Care, according to a *Kline Market Research, 2015.*

So much of *Evolving Beauty* speaks to Multi-Cultural haircare Along with the *evolving* spirit of the industry, this book honors the nuances and sensibilities of women of color who represent serious purchasing power, particularly as it relates to haircare. There is a haircare focus for two reasons: first, Multi-Cultural women reportedly consume nine times more than their General Market counterparts *(Nielson, 2015)*. Secondly, I love everything about haircare—especially how a new style can make a woman look and feel completely brand new, instantly raising her self-esteem. The book, *Queens*, (Alexander & Cunningham, 2005) photo captures women from across the globe. A trinity of black women, hair, and beauty salons: *Portraits of Black Women and Their Fabulous Hair.* The book highlights the impact hair has from women across the globe from the African Diaspora.

The Multi-Cultural haircare industry is wildly underestimated. Mintel, a market research firm, estimates the market value of hair care made for the Multi-Cultural consumer is **$774 million**, projected to reach **$876 million by 2019** (Mintel, 2015) Not bad, but there are a few missing components to this projected sales number. First, General Market brands (ethnic consumers purchasing General Market brands and vice versa). Secondly— weaves and wigs. Lastly, independent beauty supply stores, distributors, direct sales, e-commerce, styling tools and accessory devices. If all of these were included, the sales could triple to over a trillion (Opiah, 2014). It's also imperative to note that the Multi-Cultural woman has an especially intrinsic relationship with her hair. These additional components and sales represent an introspective view of her world—and also, how the world sees her. Hefty haircare sales represent the cultural importance hair to the African American and Multi-Cultural woman.

In 2001, I was the Brand Manager working on Johnson Product's Gentle Treatment (GT) Relaxer Kit. It was my job to restage and refresh GT (a 20-year old heritage brand) with new packaging, a reinforced positioning, and to develop opportunities to attract a new, younger demographic. The advertising mediums were print, outdoor advertising, radio and direct mail—with two major integrated campaigns. One was around Mother's Day, The Freedom to Do, ™ utilizing heavy radio and print. The other was an experiential campaign with coupon redemption and a trial-to-support partnership with an emerging national property, Black Cinema Café (operated by Film Life , Inc., owners of American Black Film Festival [ABFF]).

I had a young (under 30-year-old), smart manager, LeRon McKendrick-Grier. A savvy new Director, fresh from big brands like Neutrogena and Soft-Sheen Carson. As an Intrepreneur, corporate culture and brand autonomy are dictated by your manager's maturity, their sensibilities, confidence level and position. Their intelligence and knowledge of marketing and communication is vital to your corporate experience. I learned a lot from LeRon, especially her ability to successfully navigate with foresight, corporate politics. She's gifted in that sense. LeRon was a critical catalyst to building a solid foundation of understanding in the ethnic beauty industry. We became fast friends, forever 911 sisters — having spent three days together in the wake of the "911" tragedy, in 2011.

The Gentle Treatment refresh went well and the brand grew in dollars and units. In retrospect, I can't imagine restaging a brand today without a digital component. In today's age, if you don't have digital, you don't exist.

I managed the development of the the first Gentle Treatment website ever. Digital advertising was just emerging (as foreign as cable television) when the brand was restaged. Not only was digital omitted from the integrated campaign (I do remember considering digital ads), but there was very little data to support going off the beaten path from mainstream advertising of print, radio and TV. It would have been an Intrapreneurial risk I wasn't prepared to take. The tactics used to gain and maintain market share today are completely different than they were in the pre-digital and pre-digital advertising era.

Top 10 Ethnic Hair Care Manufacturers			
7/1/01	COT: FDM	2/1/15	COT: MULO
Total Sales $250 Million	Share	Total Sales $542 Million	Share
1 SoftSheen/Carson	28.60%	Sundial Creations	12.10%
2 Luster	12.20%	SoftSheen/Carson	11.50%
3 Proline/Alberto-Culver	12.10%	Namaste Labs	8.70%
4 Revlon/A.P.	9.40%	Lusters	5.60%
5 Johnson Products	5.60%	Strength of Nature	5.40%
6 J.M Products	4.50%	Unilever	4.90%
7 Bronner Brothers	4.40%	Colomer USA	4.00%
8 J. Strickland	1.70%	Advanced Beauty Systems Inc.	3.90%
9 Advanced Research Labs	1.70%	Proctor & Gamble	3.90%
10 Namaste Labs	1.70%	Cheatham Chemical Co.	3.90%
Mfgs. with less than 1.7% (18.1% total share)		Mfg. with less than 3.9% (36.1% total share)	

Figure 3 IRI Data, 2001 and 2015.
COT: Class of Trade
Chart Design: Shine Beauty Culture Consultancy

The **Top 10 Ethnic Hair Care Manufacturers** from 2001 to 2015, with sales of $250 million to $542 million, as reported by IRI—a leading retail data reporting system. IRI reports consumer sales from retailers via UPC product scans.

The industry suggests there is another 50 percent of sales that aren't accounted for, derived from beauty supply stores, commonly known in the beauty industry as over-the-counter (OTCs). This is compelling because it essentially doubles the manufacturer sales. It's important to note that beauty supply estimates are direct ship estimates and do not account for consumer sales. *More on consumer sales in chapters to come.*

The **Top 10 Ethnic Hair Care Manufacturers** chart summarizes change in the top manufacturers, the increase in haircare sales and retail inclusion, along with the rise of independent manufacturers with brands that focus on The New Naturals Movement. Over the past 15 years, the market has expanded into what was commonly known as "FDM," and has now become "MULO." FDM represents Food, Drug and Mass retail outlets and doesn't include channels like Walmart, Club and Dollar Stores. In 2012, Walmart decided to include their data again (as in the 1990s), which the IRI terms MULO, for Multi Outlet and Nielsen. Another big data benchmark reporting company in the Beauty Industry terms it "xAOC" (eXtended All Outlet Combined). "FDMx" stands for Food, Drug and Mass Walmart. The 2001 sales data does NOT include Walmart [iv]. *More on retail sales channels of distribution in chapters to come.*

For almost two decades, large global manufacturers have acquired and sold African American (AA) Heritage Companies such as Soft Sheen/Carson (owned by L'Oreal since 1998) and Johnson Products, once an icon brand—now an orphan brand. Johnson has been acquired and sold multiple times from IVAX, to Soft-Sheen Carson, to L'Oreal, Wella Corporation, Proctor & Gamble again, the with Eric and Renee Brown (Renee a former Pro-Line Executive). Today (2016) the brand is with Dr. Miracles.

Ethnic Hair Care by Category					
	2001			**2015**	
	CLASS OF TRADE: FDM			CLASS OF TRADE: MULO	
	Total Sales $250 Million	$ Dollar Sales in Millions	Percent (%) of Market Share	Total Sales $541 Million	$ Dollar Sales in Millions	% of Market Share
1	Adult Relaxers	$55.90	22.40%	Styling Aids	$162.00	30%
2	Hair dress	$41.80	16.70%	Conditioner	$87.80	16%
3	Ethnic Hair Color	$39.50	15.80%	Hair Dressing	$83.00	15%
4	Styling	$36.80	14.80%	Adult Relaxer	$69.80	13%
5	Conditioner	$20.50	8.20%	Shampoo	$43.20	8%
6	Curl/Wave	$16.20	6.50%	Ethnic Hair Color	$36.90	7%
7	Children's Relaxer	$10.00	4.00%	Children's Hair Care	$10.30	7%
8	Men's Styling	$9.30	3.70%	Men's Hair Care	$13.30	2%
9	Texturizer Kits	$9.00	3.70%	Children's Relaxer	$10.30	2%
10	Shampoo	$7.10	2.80%	Curl/Wave	$9.80	2%
11	Children's Styling	$3.70	1.50%	Texturizer Kits	$8.20	2%

Figure 4, Source: IRI Data, 2001 and 2015.

The **Ethnic Hair Care by Category** chart conveys the significance of the *natural haircare trend,* a movement of over the 15 years plus. In 2001, relaxers were the number one product in ethnic haircare. Today, even with the inclusion of major retailers like Walmart and Dollar Chains (Family Dollar and Dollar General), adult relaxers have lost more than half in sales.

The transformation of product category by styling aids, conditioners and oils, signify the plethora of products and sub-products being utilized by *The Natural Hair Movement* to maintain and style natural hair. Conditioners are the leading product class. They've grown since 2001 in market share by 22 percent, the exact percentage adult relaxers held in market share in 2001. Deep conditioners (rinse-out), leave- in conditioners, treatments, gels, mousses, crèmes, aerosol and non-aerosol sprays, lotions, spritz and holding products, petrolatums, polishes, oils and serums comprise these top three product categories. "Naturalistas (consumers that engage in The Natural Hair Movement) will tell you that product assortment and manufacturers are endless. In the pursuit of beautiful hair, consumers continually seek the perfect products to maintain their natural hair. Interestingly enough, all products in the category targeted to the natural hair consumer are NOT all natural, certified natural or containing natural ingredients. According to the USDA ingredients list the contents must be 95 percent or more certified organic for product stability and efficacy. The remaining five percent of the ingredients should come from an approved USDA list.

In 2001, the New Naturals haircare category did not exist in name, in IRI or Nielsen data. It wasn't segmented by premium retail shelf space as it is today. With the resurgence of natural hair consumers (revived from the 60s and 70s), important categories to recognize are the Chemical, Texture and Straightening options.

Users are not always what they seem. Although the relaxer category has decreased in dollar sales and lost market share, relaxers are still players in the overall haircare category. Adults are still relaxing their children's hair and adult consumers are using children's relaxers with the mindset that they're less damaging. Also, some men who use curl/wave texturizer kits are termed "secret users" or "closet users," according to independent research by Shine Beauty Culture Consultancy. These are the men are not comfortable acknowledging they use curl, wave or event hair color (chemical) products.

Ethnic Hair Color has decreased in market share and there are a few theories to explain why. The first, is the influence of The Natural Hair Care Movement. Although many *Natutralistas* do not consider hair color a "no-no," as hair color is intended to change the color of your hair, not the texture (unless it is pre-damaged or damage suffered from the color application). Another reason ethnic hair color product usage has decreased is because ethnic or Multi-Cultural consumers are using mainstream, or General Market, hair color. It penetrates the hair deeply and lasts longer, particularly for the graying consumer. And lastly, the ethnic consumer and professional stylist have a different relationship with hair color than the general market does, as it relates to professional knowledge and application, risk of damage and proficiency in application is high.

Perhaps what is most important to note, of the two charts combined (Top Manufacturing & Top Categories; 2001 vs. 2015), is the rise and resurgence of independent haircare brands and companies driven by natural products for the new natural hair consumer.

A clear snapshot of brands in A NEW AGE OF BEAUTY:

- ➢ **Namaste Labs** was ranked No.10 in 2001, and grew to No.3 in 2015.
- ➢ **Soft Sheen** (owned by L'Oreal) has remained a top competitor and continues to grow.
- ➢ **Luster's**, a heritage brand, still ranks in the top five, and remains independently owned.
- ➢ **Sundial Creations** (absent from the reporting radar in 2001) is now the No.1 brand in the U.S., 15 years later, with robust global sales.

SOCIAL DATA IN A NEW AGE OF BEAUTY

In December 2015, WWD published The Beauty Inc. Awards to honor social media as a key driving force in beauty sales. Beauty Inc. published the top brands who most influence sales based upon ratings by earned media valuation. (WWD, 2015)

According to WWD, although all social media platforms continue to grow and explode in content, Instagram owns the fastest growth platform. (WWD, 2015) There was one brand amongst the winners that specifically stood out and exemplifies what's taking place in A NEW AGE OF BEAUTY. This highlighted brand ranked No.4 in the **Top 10 Haircare Brands** category, on the heels of industry moguls: Redken, Garnier and TRESemme, in that order. It ranked No.6 in **Top 10 Skin Care Brands**, amongst leading-edge names like Lush, Clinique, Neutrogena, Soap & Glory and The Body Shop. This brand was also awarded Corporate Social Responsibility of the Year 2015.

What is this brand with all the buzz? Shea Moisture. Founded in 1991 by Richelieu Dennis and his family, in Harlem, New York—Shea Moisture products and company pay homage to Sofi Tucker, Dennis' grandmother. A forerunner in the Beauty Industry, Tucker made and sold shea beauty products in 1912, in a market in Sierra Leone. (WWD, 2015) Today, Shea Moisture is owned by Sundial Brands.

Shea Moisture's high ranking in WWD's Beauty Inc.'s Social Media Year of the Influencer 2015, coupled with their ability to penetrate the African American target audience *and* transcend to mainstream/General Market, is momentous. This success symbolizes the synergy of THE BEAUTY BREAKTHROUGH THEOREM™ Important to note: Not only did Sundial keep original packaging intact, but the products support the Green Community as ingredients are certified organic and ethically sourced. To keep step with social responsibility, 10 percent of Shea Moisture proceeds goes to women-led businesses or The Sofi Tucker Foundation. Founder Richelieu Dennis calls it, "Community Commerce." (WWD, 2015)

Today, Shea Moisture sells hair, skin, body and face cosmetic products to people of all shades, races and ethnicities—internationally and domestically—from Walgreens to Walmart, Target to Boots, as well as many e-commerce distributors.

In 2016, Shea Moisture launched the controversial campaign, #BREAKTHEWALLS. It's a plea to remove the multi-cultural or ethnic haircare section from retail. Every retail store, grocery, drug, mass and discount stores have a specific store area, aisle or shelf as designated space for the ethnic products or multi-cultural consumers. #BREAKTHEWALLS seeks to a universal beauty product plaining field, where all brands exist together and consumer navigate as a "free for all" without ethnic disclaimer. There are pro's and con's to both scenarios. The opportunities for the small independents may be eliminated if this is realized. However, with the growing ethic, Multi-Cultural population and the cross-over appeal that exists in the beauty landscape this could be a thought leading philosophy. The verdict on this will be interesting, it's too early to tell. *More on retail distribution in chapters to come.*

A NEW AGE OF BEAUTY is an ever-evolving space of discovery within the business of beauty landscape. It offers instant digital, two-way communication between brand and consumer, along with an explosive Multi-Culturally populated terrain, predicated to support product innovation like no other era. By utilizing modern navigational tools, brands can break through the excess and enjoy success. Our proprietary algorithm, a compass for small and large brands alike, in new or existing categories, can help make smart decisions to chart a brand's next stage in the Brand Matrix. This is the essence of THE BEAUTY BREAKTHROUGH THEOREM ™.

2 KNOW THY SELF

"Know your product inside and out, before you start working and relate that knowledge to the consumer's needs."
~Bill Bernbach

"Branding" has become a buzzword in the NEW AGE OF BEAUTY for anyone selling or promoting anything. Product Managers, Brand Executives, Bloggers, Vloggers, Brand Ambassadors and Celebrity Socialites all brand their properties. How many times have you heard someone say they need to "protect their brand?" Countless, I'm sure. Brands get ONE first introduction to the public. Although I've seen new beauty brands launch in excellence. The majority perpetuate ineffective messaging, missed opportunities and wasted revenue.

Branding is a marketing strategy, an art, that establishes presence in the mind of the consumer to attract and maintain interest. Today's marketers use the word so loosely that an already complex branding process has become a multifarious practice. With a myriad of branding approaches in the marketplace, it can be daunting, if not entirely overwhelming.

Branding is one of my favorite things to do in marketing and communications. I delight in building brands to shine. At Shine Beauty Culture Brand Management Consultancy, we use a solid 3-prong approach. Our branding is timeless, built for success and longevity. We focus on **Brand Essence, Brand Communication,** and **Evolution in Branding—Innovation,** with key strategies and smart tactics.

THE 3-PRONG ESSENTIALS: *1. BRANDING*

The first and most essential branding element is, in the words of Socrates, "Know Thyself." Branding is an inside job. The more you know about your product or service, the better you'll be able to chart your course and your future. (Just like personal growth.) So what is it that you need to know about your product or service? Well, everything. The most successful and effective brands are crystal clear about who they are. They spend a great deal of time (almost obsessively) researching their public perception. These brands always want to know: "What do my consumers (or potential consumers) think about my brand?"

Branding starts from the inside out. It's imperative to decide upfront what type of brand you are and what your intention in the industry is. Keep in mind your brand and your business will and should change over the years as your company expands and matures. This understanding will keep your decision making clear and your Brand Essence strong.

Are you passionate about the product or service you're creating? Do you want to be a legendary, iconic brand? Or, is your intention to generate wealth and be acquired by a major public company for millions of dollars in the future? Either course is a personal choice, but be honest with our intention because the public can sense inauthenticity. Your brand could suffer if your corporate decisions aren't aligned with your true intentions.

Every brand, like every person, has something special that no one else has, that sets them apart. We term this **Brand Essence.**

It's the heart and soul of your brand that differentiates you from others, creating your point(s) of difference. As a product or Blogger, your brand has something unique to offer that's different from your competitors. It's your responsibility to find out what your Brand Essence is, to foster longevity and smart niche offerings.

Start with "authenticity" to create Brand Identity. Knowing your Brand Essence is essential. Live and create from this space. A "cool" logo and a "hot" tagline are vital components in the visual/creative development of your brand. Your best decisions will be built around knowing who your brand is. If you don't know, you won't be anchored to anything—which can lead to reactionary moves in the marketplace, on-the-fly decisions, and a struggle to keep up with competitors—maybe even becoming a "Me Too Copy Cat."

Partnering will not be effective either if you aren't honest about who your brand is? Or if you don't know what makes your product or service special, *Brand Essence*. Bloggers, Vloggers, Celebrity Socialites, or any other connections won't fit. All of this is avoidable and an unnecessary waste of time and money.

At Shine Beauty Culture Consultancy, our clients get to take advantage of our *Brand Essence*" series. It includes a successful series of questions, exercises and word association modules to uncover your true *Brand Essence*. The first module involves developing a list of words that represent your brand and finding common links between those words or phrases. The word association exercise is the first step toward developing an overview for your brand logo and tagline. This exercise is the inception of developing a clear vision and mission statement. Brands without clarity of vision and purpose tend to offer a discombobulated public perception. Therefore, this exercise is essential.

If you have a business plan, you've probably already done a SWOT Analysis (Strengths, Weaknesses, Opportunities and Threats evaluation). If not, now is the time to do so, to link your brand essence with positioning insight. *(more on positioning to cone)*. This will help reason and reduce the inherent risk of starting a business, be it a beauty business, or any business.

To continue refining your *Brand Essence*, we return to the word list and answer critical brand questions as part of the series. You'll want to be clear on the following: What is your big picture purpose and message? Why do you believe what you believe? Why does it matter? And, most importantly: Who will care and why should they care? As a Beauty Executive, brainstorming with Research & Development, key stakeholders, or others on the marketing team, helps support this discovery.

As hard as it may seem to figure out what's different and special about your brand, it's that little, usually simplistic element, that allows you to stand out from the crowd. Find it. Know and utilize your unique feature, benefit or niche/service offering. And then, publicize your Brand Essence, perpetually.

Be sure to understand who your consumer is. Unequivocally, the most common and costly mistake I've seen brands make, is trying to be everything to everyone. It's simply not possible. If your brand is built upon being natural and good, and you have consumer loyalty from being natural and good, but then decide to launch a product that's chock- full of chemicals — this decision goes against everything you say you are. The action becomes the antithesis of your Brand Essence. Consumers are savvy and loyal. A new chemically induced product launch will create a different opinion of your brand, most likely not a positive one. You have to weigh the risks and the benefits. Ask: Is there value in losing consumers permanently to gain financially (and immediately) from this product? Is it worth the risk and the change of reputation? There isn't a right or wrong answer. The brand may benefit, the resolution clear over time.

Lastly, uncover your Brand Value Proposition. Value Proposition is the emotional and rational benefit that customers receive from purchasing your product or service. It's the large scale core benefit within Brand Positioning. It's **what you**

promise to deliver to the consumer, why they need it, and how they'll benefit from what you're offering. Value Proposition can apply to any company, product or service.

SMART BRANDING

Brand: Philosophy, www.philosphy.com
Type: Prestige
Product: Take a Deep Breath
Brand Pillars: Skin care, Real, Aspirational, Emotional Benefits

Value Proposition
"You see life more clearly, when you take a moment to breathe."
Philosophy *spends most of its product real estate describing the emotional benefits of the product versus the product features and benefits. The product value proposition is emotionally brilliant! Everyone needs a moment to step back and see things more clearly, stop and breathe deeply. The branding connects with everyone, and so it transcends ethnicities and socio-economic barriers with smart branding tactics like this.*

AN IMPORTANT NOTE FOR BEAUTY INFLUENCERS

Beauty Influencers can (and should) apply all of the Essential Insider Tactics outlined in this chapter to their brands as well. Develop your Blogger/Vlogger Brand Essence, know and utilize your Value Proposition, and be sure to share your Brand Story (*discussion forthcoming*). As stated above, your Brand Essence shapes your brand character and defines your brand style. Therefore, choosing to work with brands that you authentically like, trust, and use, will garner genuine brand experiences and project a powerful public perception.

Brand Executives often create new products each year with

the sole purpose of generating revenue. Sure, that's why we're in business, to generate revenue. However, if the new product isn't a line extension or a new product range of value to the customer—if it's not a good fit for the brand, or well designed with strong product efficacy—then the new products won't generate long term growth. Brands often forget that existing products may just need a restage to become a hero product.

The same ethical principles apply to Beauty Influencers. Asian Make-Up Vlogger Michelle (YouTube— Dope2111) started vlogging in 2009, and now has over 3 million subscribers, with estimated monthly earnings of

$14,758.91. Bethnay Moto (YouTube—MacBarbie07) is a teen from California who also started vlogging in 2009, has over 9 million subscribers, with estimated monthly earnings of $15,781.95. (Advertising Age, 2015) Unfortunately there weren't any African American Beauty Influencers included in the top paid list. Again this is significant because African Americans over-index in beauty spending, but are not garnering the income other top bloggers in the category are receiving.

Brand Executives and consumers are left baffled, wondering which beauty brands the Influencer has an affinity for, sans the sponsored "paid" campaign. The implementation of a code of ethics for digital content creators has been in discussion for several years. It would resolve concerns surrounding: freedom of speech, honesty, stating your allegiance to stay independent, admit and correct mistakes immediately, give appropriate credit, and to verify and reveal sources, as necessary, to name a few. Most companies do not have a code of ethics for the digital content creators or influencers they partner with, though some do. Ask the brand you're working with if they have one to ensure you don't violate any of their policies. The ask will also inform the client you care about policy and integrity.

CREATE YOUR BRAND STORY

If you don't have a Brand Story, you're just another commodity or service. Stories connect people. Brand Stories build your brand and company around a narrative that people care about and want to buy into.

Stories are important in marketing and communication. Great stories make people *feel something,* and those emotions create powerful connections. Brand Stories are about framing. Shape your Brand Story so that it appeals to the consumer's emotions. This way, your value can be set as a premium, aligned with brand strengths. Stories bridge brand loyalty, with value. Brand stories create a framework that consumers can hold on to, with a strategy for growth.

An important element of brand storytelling is to continue the story. So often brands think the story is about how the brand was conceived. It isn't. It's about how you connect, and how you make your ideal customer feel. Stories have a beginning, a middle and an end. If you've been in business for 10 years, you know your business and story has changed. Brands must continue to evolve their story—and it must be as compelling and relevant to the target audience today as it was on day one.

Brand Stories are an extension of the brand essence. Brand building and should also be developed from the inside out. A great story strategy demands that you: show how your brand stands out, increase brand awareness, create customer loyalty and empower profits.

I work with brands at all stages of their development— from independent startups (creating the culture), to established brands that are restaging their positioning or developing new line extensions. The most successful brands don't operate like commodities. The maintain a strong presence and allow the branding to develop organically versus a defensive, competitor reactionary disposition.

As a Beauty Brand Manager or Beauty Influencer, it's your responsibility to give your customers a good story. It starts with a feeling and a meaning — and then, connection (or lack thereof). It's that influential moment when a customer sees your logo for the first time, then hears your brand name. She then views your website, clicks on your "about" page, or develops social media engagement with you.

Many times the "word-of-mouth" story about your brand becomes your Brand Story. Again, it should be a good story with emotional connectivity. Your Brand Essence and your Brand Story are sisters, striving for distinction and emotional appeal.

As a Beauty Influencer, you can create greater value for your campaigns starting today. Begin by speaking with authority through your blog or social media channels about your brand's story. Make them want to lean in, hear it — and most of all, feel it.

SMART BRANDING

Brand: Shea Moisture, www.sheamoisture.com
Type: Mass
Products: hair, skin, body, make-up
Brand Pillars: natural, shea butter, family legacy brand, philanthropic, African ancestry

Brand Story
Shea Moisture.com - *Sofi Tucker started selling shea nuts at the village market in Bonthe, Sierra Leone, in 1912. By age 19, the widowed mother of four was selling Shea Butter, African Black Soap and her homemade hair and skin preparations all over the countryside. Sofi Tucker was our Grandmother and Shea Moisture is her legacy.*

KNOW YOUR TARGET CONSUMER

Find out who your top consumers are. Uncover your primary, secondary and tertiary consumer through psychographic and demographic assessments. Psychographics explain "why" consumers buy. It's often termed IAO, as it includes the "Interests, Attitudes and Opinions" of consumer details like his/her lifestyle, hobbies, spending habits and values.

Demographics explain "who" is buying. Demographic profile assessments help determine the size of the market, with key population factors such as age, race, sex, economic status, level of education, income level, marital status, employment, and other factors based upon a product or service.

At Shine Beauty Culture, we create prototype levels of **who** the consumer is to illustrate the types of sensibilities that the consumer **has**. Some of this information can be garnered by using website analytics or testing for shifts in sales (pre and post special offers). For in-depth consumer discovery, a customized research study is required. Your consumer shifts as your brand matures, so identifying who your consumer is will help anchor your brand and support future master plans. *More on uncovering your target audience in Chapter 3.*

SMART BRANDING

Brand: The WonderKer, Keratin Infused Pillow Case,
www.thewonderker.com

Type: Prestige

Product: Haircare

Brand Pillars: natural, keratin infused, silk, hair maintenance, hair routine, prestige, premium quality

Brand Essence, Branding, Logo

Challenge: The brand name and imagery were disconnected from the prestige vision of the brand and luxury price point. A brand redesign can be risky. It is important to keep existing customers and gain new consumers as a result of the changes.

Result

Through ideation, an online questionnaire, A/B testing and brand analysis the logo name and tag line were re-designed to reflect the prestige price point and brand name. From the Pillow Bonnet (an antiquated name, associated with southern hair practices) to: a modern name and design that highlights a prestige product name, and image, aligned with the product and features and benefits.

SMART BRANDING

Courtesy: Sunny Isle Jamaican Black Castor Oil - Graphic: Michael Jackson

Brand: Sunny Isle Jamaican Black Castor Oil, www.sunnyislejamaicanblackcastoroil.com

Type: Mass

Product: Haircare

Brand Pillars: Healthy, Natural, Original, Authenticity

Brand Essence, Point of Difference

Challenge

The brand was in Pre-Star stage and did not have a unique brand image, brand essence or point of difference.

Result

Through in-depth brand discovery it was determined that Sunny Isle is the only JBCO that's been approved for export by the Jamaican Government. There are many Jamaican Black Castor Oil competitors in the marketplace. However, Sunny Isle is the only JBCO that can make this point of distinction. A branded banner was developed.

THE 3-PRONG ESSENTIALS:

2. BRAND COMMUNICATION

Brand Messaging is the most important tactic in speaking with consumers. The conversation should be just that — a dialogue between brand and audience, a 2-way exchange. The goal is to captivate the audience so that consumers want to respond back in the many "call to action" avenues devised specifically for this purpose within the campaign. All communication should have an end goal prior to implementation.

The message should extend from the Brand Essence and appeal to the ever evolving demographic of the target audience and the population. Effective communication should include conversations that are frequent, consistent and seamless.

Once you develop your campaign theme and positioning (through continual research and feedback), you'll want to follow *The 3 C's of Campaign Communication:* Be Clear, Compelling and Consistent. Clarity lends itself to brevity. Keep your message short, clear and to the point. Don't use complex words or difficult phrases. Your message should be relevant and compelling. Relevant to the target age and interest, and compelling to ignite consumer emotions, so they feel and are moved to get involved. The consumer should want to react to the campaign by responding to the call-to-actions (web, mobile, QR code, in-store, social media, or other) as they're created for this purpose. *More on Campaigns in chapters to come.*

SMART BRANDING

Brand Messaging & Campaigns
Brand: Proctor & Gamble Brands,
                         www.pgeveryday.com
Type: Mass
Products: A variety: Haircare, Body, Skincare
Campaign Pillars: Connectivity to consumer, reinforces that
                         Black is Beautiful and Valued.

My Black is Beautiful - #MBIB
My Proctor & Gamble's My Black is Beautiful Campaign, established in 2008. The campaign has evolved but is still running today. The #MyBlackIsBeautiful community celebrates everything that makes them beautiful, from the inside out. Join the #MBIB conversation! www.myblackisbeautiful.com.

This campaign is smart branding—it's integrates social media (Facebook-over 2.5M followers, twitter and youtube), as well as experiential events. It resonates with consumers and is particularly unique because it transcends age through the African American female community. Several brands are embraced in the campaign under the Proctor & Gamble umbrella to include: CoverGirl® Queen Collection, Crest®, Olay®, Definity, Pantene Pro-V® and Secret®

THE 3-PRONG ESSENTIALS:

3. EVOLUTION & INNOVATION

Evolution and Innovation are key in building successful beauty brands. And so this book, *Evolving Beauty*, speaks directly to that. The Beauty Industry will always evolve. Consumer interests, products, services and utilities, will continually change and grow as brands expand and mature. To evolve, brands need innovation within transformation — in both messaging and product development. Innovation is the single most important way to distinguish your brand as a "beauty-forward brand." It's also the easiest way to capture new consumers, through smart branding.

I've seen countless inexperienced companies develop initial strategies with no room for messaging or product range to grow. It's mystifying. Innovation is developed through brand and consumer research. It's that never ending discovery of your public perception, the connection you have with the consumer's wants and needs. Sometimes it's a need the consumer wants, but isn't even aware of yet.

The demand for consistent modernizing of messaging can't be reinforced enough. Brand copy must be adjusted, and fine- tuned, and then adjusted again, but within the "right" timing. This is based upon **THE BEAUTY BREAKTHROUGH THEOREM ™** , *see Chapter 1 The Business of Beauty in a NEW AGE for a comprehensive explanation.*

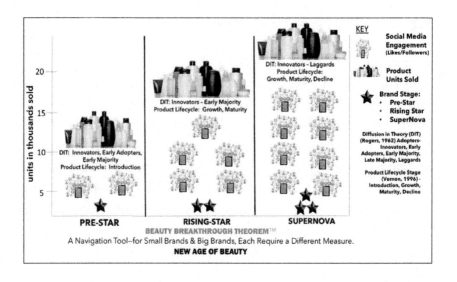

It takes time to build a brand to shine. Building beauty brands is a process that's multi-layered with information and procedures that require individual and collective consideration. The branding process isn't an easy one and should not be rushed. Branding requires expert skills and a healthy dose of creativity.

Pursue inspiration everywhere. Beauty lives and breathes in all people, places, and things. Be cognizant of the product lifecycles and brand stages, *as outlined in Chapter 1.* All are to be considered in the development stage. Use the Beauty Breakthrough Theorem™ to assess if it's a good time to change your logo or add a tag line. Evaluate factors like social media engagement, Brand Stage, units sold as a relationship to consumer relevance. Understand that you may attract the early adopters, with a brand change, but the late majority will take more time to penetrate with new ness or changes.

Use the Beauty Breakthrough Theorem ™ as a tool to evaluate your brand and determine if now is the time to break through the clutter, into the beauty landscape with your brand.

3 SOCIAL RESEARCH

"The more you know,
the more you know, you don't know."
~ Macy Gray

Discovery is an act, a process we enjoyed every day as kids. Back then, we were able to go outside and play all day long. We were encouraged to "get lost," to find something new, as long as we got home before the street lights came on. We discovered people, places and things that were foreign. We uncovered parts of life unthought-of or unknown before.

It's important to offer a sense of macro discovery to a brand and the audience that fuels it — not to mention the audience it hasn't connected with yet. Audiences who aren't aware they want your product — yet.

As a Brand Manager, ask the following three questions: 1) Who is my target audience and what do they care about? 2) What are the industry trends that are driving purchase decisions? 3) What competitive edge do my competitors have over my brand? If you don't know the answers to these brand questions, you need to begin the process of discovery and research as soon as possible.

CULTURE

In today's New Age of Beauty, research is evolving along with the speed of technology and the implications related to cultural cues, are also evolving, as they correspond with purchase decisions. Culture helps define and direct strategies for brands.

Traditional definitions of culture speak to generational behaviors of specific ethnic groups and their behavior. Today's definition is a combination of sensibilities, interests, patterns, routines and habits. Culture defies categories and segmentations. In A NEW AGE OF BEAUTY, culture is not defined by generational groups or traditions.

CULTURE [kuhl-cher] (Dictionary.Reference.com)

1. the behaviors and beliefs characteristic of a particular social, ethnic, or age group:
2. the sum total of ways of living built up by a group of human beings and transmitted from one generation to another.
3. the total range of activities and ideas of a group of people with shared traditions, which are transmitted and reinforced by members of the group
4. the socially transmitted behavior patterns, beliefs, attitudes and values of a particular time period, class, community or population. (Dictionary.Reference.com)

As discussed in the *Brand Essence* previous chapter, building an effective beauty brand requires an in- depth knowledge and understanding of the who and what your brand is. Including the *audience* and the *consumer thought process as it relates to purchase and usage trends* — as well as the bigger vision and awareness of the *Beauty Industry* — with a comprehension of the competitive landscape. New start-ups and established brands alike should maintain beauty-forward strategies as a priority to maintain relevance and continue to gain market share.

Building Brand Essence is essential for beauty- forward growth whether you're working with a startup or restaging an established brand. Expanding to create a fresh message or current tagline to connect with a specific target audience (or subculture) is a perpetual requirement if you want to stay relevant in today's ever-evolving business of beauty.

How do we do this? **Research.** We must learn to watch, listen, hear, and understand consumer wants and needs. Watch what they do, listen to what they say, hear what they don't say, and understand (process) it all.

Exploring the audience and getting to know how they live within a larger community will unveil prominent patterns, ideologies and critical cultural cues. In essence, you need to know the Hatfields **and** the McCoys. Try to understand your competitors. Delve into their psychographic and demographic archetype compositions. Get to know how people live. This is so key in making successful brand decisions. Research uncovers otherwise elusive trends that direct future strategies. It's understanding the present so you can meet it in the future.

Research is the process, or systematic discovery, of new knowledge, beyond what's already known. It's the emergence of new intelligence as it relates to a brand, a problem, an underlying reason or behavioral trait. Uncover trends, thoughts or opinions, and then design, execute and analyze to reinforce change and to tip the hand of the brand's next course of action.

BRAND EXECUTIVES SHOULD HAIL RESEARCH?

Throughout my 15 plus years of working with Beauty Corporations and Agencies, and as an Entrepreneur and a Beauty Consultant, the single most ignored, overlooked, least developed, under-utilized and discounted component of brand building, without debate is: **Data and Research**. IRI, Nielsen, Mintel or EuroMonitor International, are the most well-known and respected research organizations in the global beauty industry. They offer tremendous insight through sales and consumer data on an annual and quarterly basis.

Please understand, there are consequences in failing to conduct research to confirm consumer interests, brand concepts, brand names, positioning, taglines, value proposition, packaging, advertising and promotional messages. As a Brand Manager, you're responsible for the health and success of a brand or a portfolio of brands. It's just not prudent or fiscally responsible to skip research. The stakes are too high and the beauty industry and categories are too competitive to omit it. Plus, having data to support at least a portion of your decisions will show key stakeholders you're prudent.

But, it's done more times than not, with indie brand and established brands alike, the research component is skipped. If research shows the opposite of the desired launch direction, there could be corporate pitfalls in missed launches and wasted money and resources. Unfortunately, one of the reasons for the lack of research, is senior management with temperament and ego. When the ego prevails, senior executives believe they already know what the consumer desires and they refuse to entertain the cost or time it takes to research, to test or course-correct. The Brand Manager is then forced as her responsibility to explain the risks involved in launching new brands without garnering comprehensive qualitative and quantitative consumer research. Providing intelligent data to senior management that supports the launch or campaign budget defines you as trusted professional and prudent manager. Honor your position with complete integrity, it's a valuable position to be in and the rewards can be bountiful when stakeholders believe you have the brand in vested interest.

I've seen C-Suite Executives (CEOs, VPs, usually Director and above) test new packaging new product concepts, advertising and other messaging, simply by throwing the products against the wall and hoping they stick. They do this based on limitations related to time, resources, staff labor or other budgetary constraints. They don't conduct internal research, nor do they hire external experts. Whether you have a launching new brand as a start-up or as a corporate giant (whether you have a big or small budget) it means taking a risk. There's always a gamble with brand reputation, finances and resources, in launching new products — and zero guarantees.

Brand Managers have autonomy to act as if the brand were their own. Intrapreneurs working for large corporations are most likely managing billion-dollar P&L (profit and loss) statements. Because of this, I strongly suggest all research reports, requests, denials and risk assessments are archived for reference. As an Entrepreneur serving as Brand Manager, the same rules apply: fiscal responsibility is paramount.

Brand managers seek hard, solution-driven data to create innovation, fill market voids, correct challenges, complete or compliment portfolios, and ultimately, to gain the lead in market share. Brand research not only provides sober business data to make effective decisions, but it gives deep insight into consumer minds. The tricky thing is, consumers don't always behave the way they say they will or do. In fact, when it comes to consumer behavior and buying decisions, consumers *rarely* walk their talk.

YOUR RESEARCH SHOULD BEGIN HERE

An excellent starting point for research is Market Analysis/Competitive Analysis to better understand where your brand is in relationship to competitors. Then, followed by brand testing (packaging, imaging and product efficacy). In previous chapters we discussed the importance of identifying Brand Essence, an interpersonal relationship of sorts; the brand's discovery of itself, from the inside out. Research is the opposite. It is the interpersonal relationship, the bond and perspective of the brand held from the outside, by the audience; an outside view of how others see you. As a marketer, you have to have an intrinsic relationship with the market landscape, of how other brands are perceived by consumers, as well as your own. This perspective relates to pricing, features and benefits, brand essence, point of difference, distribution, experiential and promotional events, as well as value proposition.

Consider:

> ➢ How is your brand best positioned, and alongside competitors?
> ➢ Can you offer the promise consumers want and need— even if you don't know what's happening in the market place?

If you can't then that's where Brand Research comes in. It's vital that focus be directed toward peripheral competitive brand knowledge, and while maintaining your own brand course.

Let's go deeper. Questions to consider regarding your niche market:

> ➢ *Which brands have the highest independent awareness levels?*
> ➢ *What words or cultural cues do consumers associate with other brands in the market?*
> ➢ *What do consumers like or dislike about those brands?*
> ➢ *What do consumers wish existed within those brands on the market today? (What's the unmet need?)*

By clearly identifying both pain and power points within the brand—consumer wants and needs. Brands can better determine how to find opportunity in meeting those needs.

AUDIENCE ANALYSIS

Brand Development Research requires this: You must know who your audience is. It's imperative to determine the three tiers of your target market (primary, secondary and tertiary audiences). Know who will buy your brand, and who will buy it most frequently. Once you identify your primary audience, explore the sub-groups that have similar behavior (the secondary and tertiary groups). Understanding consumer *behavior* and group segmentations enables informed decision making for successful marketing and social communication campaigns.

Notice the word "behavior" is used versus "demographic profile." In A NEW AGE OF BEAUTY, behavior correlates to culture, as earlier defined. To flesh out and segment a target audience, you want to understand the demographic profile of a consumer group or sub-group to include: age, sex, income, gender, household size and education. Demographic profiles seek information about consumer purchasing habits to identify how often a consumer purchases a type of product. The data gathered allows the business to shape future marketing or product campaigns toward key groups of individuals, the segmented target audience. Consumer cultural sensibilities and interests dictate consumer behavior.

While demographics can be very useful in media buying and secondary marketing activities, they cannot be used to supplement other strategies or alignments. This is where research becomes so vital. Demographics should **not** be the primary focus in audience segmentation. Your research should begin with identifying: What people buy in your market, How much they spend, How often, Where they buy, and If they demonstrate brand loyalty.

To better understand consumer behavior, let's go deeper still and ask:

> ➢ *Why do consumers choose not to buy other brands?*
> ➢ *Why do consumers choose one brand over another?*
> ➢ *Why do consumers buy frequently or infrequently?*

> ➤ *Why do consumers buy in a specific store?*
> ➤ *How do consumers use the brands they buy?*
> ➤ *When do consumers use the brands they buy?*
> ➤ *How do consumers make the decision to make the actual purchase?*

If you don't know the answers, do the research to find out.

Once you segment your audience into "similar behavior" groups, you can create messages, promotions, and other campaigns that appeal to them and motivate call-to- action(s). You can also add demographic criteria into your behavioral segments to find sub-segments for clearly defined advertisements and promotional tactics.

SMART BRANDING

Brand: Ubiquitous Expo, www.UbiquitousExpo.com
Type: Open to the Public, Fee Entry
Products: A tradeshow for women, beauty vendors
Pillars: When women stand together they become more powerful, legacy building, entreprenuerial.

Branding Research Case Study
Brand: Ubiquitous Hair & Health Trade Show[1] changed its name in 2016 to Ubiquitous Expo.

Challenge: The show is more than just a Hair and Health trade show, therefore the show name and show offerings were disconnected, also the show was built as a destination place. Therefore, Washington, DC was also added to the show logo.

For the first two years, the event was named "*Ubiquitous Hair & Health Trade Show....Where Relaxed Meets Natural Hair.*" After

---

[1] In 2016, Ubiquitous Expo will celebrate it's 3rd year.

consumer research, we discovered that the attendee considered Ubiquitous more than just a hair show. Findings revealed the Ubiquitous platform inspired, motivated, promoted collaboration and encouraged women to work together to build stronger legacies for their families

Result
In 2016 the show changed its name TO: Ubiquitous Expo…Together We Are Ubiquitous`

AUDIENCE SEGMENTATION CORE VALUES

1. B2B – Beauty Manufacturers — the vendors
2. B2C – Beauty Enthusiasts
   - Age Range, House Hold Income,
   - Lifestyle Musical Interest
     o Gospel Music
     o R&B/Pop Culture

TYPES OF RESEARCH METHODS

There are two types of research: *Qualitative and Qualitative research* seeks to enrich an understanding of underlying reasons and motivations. It wants to gain insight into a problem and then dive deeper into a challenge to generate ideas or uncover thought trends. It's often followed by *quantitative research* for confirmation of discovered hunches and ideologies.

Qualitative methodologies include ethnographic, naturalistic, anthropological, field, or participant observer research. Common qualitative collection methods include focus groups (group discussions), individual interviews (one- on-one) and participation/observations. The sample size, or number of respondents, is typically small and loosely structured.

(SnapSurveys, 2016)

Quantitative research involves numbers, figures, statistics and data that counts the number of respondents that have the same generalized interests. It measures the incidence of various views and opinions. Qualitative data generalizes results from the population of interest. Common quantitative collection methods include: online questionnaires, street, mall intercepts and telephone interviews.

Qualitative research is conclusive. Meaning, it measures a large sample size of randomly selected respondents to avoid a potential bias of selected qualitative research. Qualitative research is a strongly recommended final supplement to quantitative research, to confirm a brand's course of action. (Discover Anthropology, 2015)

WHAT IS ETHNOGRAPHY?

Ethnography is a research method of qualitative research that helps to better understand consumer behavior and improve communication, marketing, sales, effectiveness, and new product development and design. (Market Research Association, 2015) The emphasis of ethnographic research is to describe and interpret a cultural or social group. Ethnographic research became prominent in the U.S. by pioneers Frank Boas and Ruth Benedict in the early 1920s. Social, or cultural, anthropology stresses the coherence of cultures by including their rules of behavior, language, material creations and ideas about the world. It also includes the need to understand each on its own terms. (Discover Anthropology, 2015) Boas trained renowned author and fellow social anthropologist, Zora Neale Hurston. *Hurston is considered one of the pre-eminent writers of the twentieth- century African-American literature.* She wrote four novels and two books of folklore based upon her extensive anthropological research — all of which have become invaluable

resources of African American oral culture.
(ZoraNealeHurston, 2015)

It's no wonder Hurston is known as the "Foremother of Interpretive Anthropology." Anthropologist Irma McLaurin notes, "Hurston's research was deeply rooted in a Diaspora paradigm, which stressed an examination of the cultural continuities and differences that emerged when Blacks were scattered across the Americas and Europe as a consequence of slavery." Zora Neale Hurston departed from convention by theorizing the African Diaspora with methodological innovations. Hurston's metaphor of anthropology as a spy-glass, as an illuminating lens and unique vision to the world, still resonates today. McClaurin and others have hailed Hurston's role as "an important innovator in anthropological theory and method." (Research University of Florida, 2015)

Unlike traditional market researchers who ask specific, highly practical questions, anthropological researchers who practice ethnography visit consumers in their homes, offices, neighborhoods and communities to observe and listen in a non-directed way. The goal is to watch and hear people's behavior on *their* terms, not yours. (Harvard Business Review, 2009) Ethnography has proven itself to be so valuable that corporate ethnographers are becoming widespread. Intel Corporation may have one of the largest corporate ethnographer internal staffs, employing over two dozen anthropologists and other trained ethnographers.

Ethnography studies deliver insights and strategies to help guide decisions of companies by providing products and services to consumers and businesses. Although it is a traditional method of studying people, the fundamental practice is still an excellent method, layered with more contemporary and modern research practices.

INSIDER RESEARCH METHODS

Our research approach at Shine Beauty Culture Consultancy, is to combine various research methods to equip Brand Executives with significant consumer insight and key cultural cues to make the best brand decisions that that will gain instant credibility and support from stakeholders. We integrate emic ethnography (questionnaires designed via digital surveys) with industry standard data (IRI, Nielsen, Mintel, EuroMonitor International) to provide a comprehensive qualitative and quantitative research analysis with reporting and recommendations.

BEAUTY INFLUENCERS + RESEARCH

WHY & HOW?
As a Blogger, Vlogger or Celebrity Influencer, your ability to increase your value, offerings and revenue with beauty clients is endless. Research is a great place to begin. Brands are interested in working with you because of the breadth of your audience and the depth of your network. They want to connect, inform and convert people through you and your trusted, authentic voice. Understanding the power of the connection to your audience and your value to a brand is paramount.

I'm a strong advocate of social media as a legitimate source for consumer insight. Social media can garner a robust sample size (hundreds to thousands) of consumer response on a variety of topics including: product efficacy, category intel, ingredients preference, usage patterns or other beauty questions — in a matter of minutes. Social Media Research (SMR) has the ability to deliver a keen perspective on what shapes consumer decisions. When a Brand Manager has a hunch or a concept they'd like to pursue, a great preliminary gauge before moving onto product development and ultimately a multi-million-dollar campaign, is via a social media post, a blog post or an expert designed questionnaire survey segmented through an email list. Depending on the sample size (number of respondents), digital surveys could satisfy quantitative research. Garnering preliminary research through Beauty Influencers to gauge consumer interest and overall perspective is an excellent and cost effective method to gauge the viability of an idea or concept.

Nevertheless, it's critical to understand that Social Media Research is not the cure-all. It should be layered in supplement with various other research methodologies. It should never serve as a substitute for consumer satisfaction or comprehensive findings.

I am not suggesting, as a Beauty Influencer, that qualitative (qual) or quantitative (quant) research or analysis is a service to offer. If you're trained or have experience with research questionnaire design, interviews or focus groups— then, yes, sure proceed. But generally, qualitative and quantitative methodologies, data analysis, along with executive-level analysis and report writing, should be reserved for research experts. Few Beauty Influencers have this skill set. If they did, they'd probably be a researcher and not an awesome Beauty Influencer like the one you are (or are becoming).

CLEAR + SIMPLE

RESEARCH QUESTIONS + SOCIAL ANALYTICS
As a Beauty Influencer, you have built-in tools to share with your clients as added value or "a la carte" service offerings. Keep your research offerings simple and your analytic reporting automated. Be sure to note your ability to report tangible insights about **your** followers. Use methods you can execute easily. This can be as simple as a blog post, as intermediate as a one question survey posted on your blog or

website, or as complex as an expert designed survey distributed to your email mailing list where you post the URL link to distribute to your consumers. Offer each of these methods with different tiers of fees associated with them. You may want to offer the simple or intermediate offering as a complimentary added bonus to show appreciation for their business or as an opportunity to form a long term relationship.

Suppose a brand is developing a new, innovative haircare multi-purpose product. For example, a wrap foam that accelerates hair drying time. The client may want to use your influencer audience to gauge a variety of inquiries throughout the process—from ideation to packaging, to advertising/promotional campaign options. The "peripheral testing" options are vast. Peripheral testing is the term used at Shine Beauty Culture Consultancy for Social Media Research that provides shape, framework and context to consumer decisions and interests.

This type of research could examine the concept of multi-purpose products, inquire about preferred ingredients, conduct A/B package design analysis, define bottle type, disc top or funnel nozzle, etc. The baseline inquiries are endless. The peripheral consumer research and response, coupled with other methods of qualitative and quantitative inquiry, builds brands with consumer insight at a fraction of the cost.

DELIVERING SIMPLE ANALYTICAL METRICS

Lastly, and perhaps the most important method in campaigns and research, is the ability to measure and deliver reporting efforts. The first step to social media measurement is knowing which measurements matter the most. Every brand has different goals, and therefore, a different measurement focus. The measurement matrix options are endless. Before research begins, determine brand "must haves." If your analytics provide those—great. If not, offer standard options that steer away from critical thinking or analysis. Utilize items you can extract from open ended questions or a survey with automated results. By using Google Analytics, you can include data from: mobile use, demographic area, time of usage, time spent on web pages, etc. This snapshot of information allows brands to analyze using their own measurement goals to get the most value from their research.

Reporting and survey design is the area research experts become uncomfortable with social media consumer research. Social media "likes," re-tweets and shares fail to provide definitive business measurements that translate into potential purchasers or actual purchases. There's also the potential for human error—although, qualitative comments from consumers can be measured for interest, usage and purchasing behavior.

Earlier I suggested an intermediate discovery research method with a one-question survey. A survey that lives on the blog home page will yield measurable quantitative results. A percentage of the following could be polled and measured: "Yes, I would use this product," "I'm interested in this product," or "No, I would not use this product," as examples of options. Of the 200 polled respondents in the example, 85 percent (170 respondents) said "Yes, I would use this product." Also, measurable qualitative research (comments from your brand inquiry post on social media) can be reviewed and analyzed at a rudimentary level. Simply tally the positive or negative responses and add up the total. The quantitative research automatically delivers percentages when the survey is closed. No analysis or critical thinking is required—nor do I advise it. There are so many variables involved within the measurement and analysis goals that it's best to simply extract the data "as is."

If brands opt for a more complex survey or expert designed questionnaire, simply post the survey URL link on the social network where you have the most engagement, for the highest number of respondents. Also, continue drawing from Google Analytics or any of the social media tracking tool (Buffer, Hootsuite, Iconosquare, etc.) to gain even more cultural cues and insight into demographic profiles. A one to two page Social Media Research report with the extracted analysis will give your client invaluable insight for their concept or product idea. It will also strengthen your partnership and provide a beautiful monetizing research opportunity as a Beauty Influencer.

To sum up the relevance and importance of research in A NEW AGE OF BEAUTY, it is and will remain one of the most important first steps in building a successful brand. Social research is here, and here to stay. I predict that in the near future social analytics will become the norm. I imagine social and web tools embedded as routine guides in web and Blogger platforms, created as tools of measurement to develop and support a brand's course of action and campaign decisions.

4 BE YOUR OWN MASTER

"Know thyself, know thy enemy.
A thousand battles, a thousand victories."
~Sun Tzu

In 2007, I decided it was time to strike out on my own and create some sweat equity for myself. Shine Exposition (SE) was my first "official" endeavor. There'd been countless previous attempts in events, health & beauty, and jewelry— but I've always returned to the beauty industry. SE had the largest capital investment to start and I'd expended great effort toward it. It began as a beauty trade show hosted by the Indiana Black Expo (IBE) in Indianapolis, IN. IBE's partnership goal with SE was to drive traffic to the show, a destination event.

Although I had three other business partners with separate roles, I was the most enthusiastic and exerted the most energy toward the business. SE was developed based on my love for beauty, my interest in the trade show industry, knowledge of beauty brands and a skill set for managing people and projects. The common denominator in the concept and positioning was me. But it was my ego—and my inability to implement the tactics that I ensure are in place for decision making with my clients and the corporations I work with—that caused us to stumble.

In short, we decided to produce a trade show in another state (we were NYC-based at the time), in our first year of business, where we didn't have a network or strong following. So when I speak of C-Suite Executive egos, not only have I worked them first hand in corporations, but I've been one of them myself.

Needless to say, tens of thousands of dollars (a substantial amount for a small business) were lost because of an inability to "know thyself." Thyself, in this context, being the brand—who the brand is, and who it wants to become. You must understand the brand you're founding and why (so you can know how) to develop it.

If I'd consulted with my own consultancy (Shine Exposition, at that time), I would've advised us to rethink our value proposition. Our offering to the consumer and spend more time in research within the industry—dig deeper and re-evaluate the partnership entirely. I would have suggested rethinking destination event. Was it based upon consumer need, consumer want, or personal ego—and then ask what value is being provided through the experience.

I'm pleased with where and how Shine Exposition has evolved, as a Boutique Beauty & MarComm Consultancy, helping small and big businesses succeed. Had we defined and cultivated our Brand Essence, yellow flags may have waved at half-staff. Had rudimentary research and competitive positioning analysis been conducted, red flags may have soared full staff—or would they? That was nine years ago. People and business models have changed and evolved to adapt to modern times and modern practices. Today, Shine Exposition may have been likened to the Bronner Brothers International Trade Show (Est. in 1947) or the Ubiquitous Expo (Est. 2014), or even better— a rendition of what was the best Shine Exposition it could have been, in our own unique Brand Essence.

Needless to say, evolution will can and will occur regardless. But an inability "to know thyself" can cost a way higher price than spending time in research, properly analyzing the business, using appropriate navigation tools, and assessing the value proposition being offered.

In short, be aware of decision motivation—whether it's ego driven or brand intelligence based.

WHAT IS A BRAND MASTER?

A Brand Master is a business owner who works to create a successful business and operational foundation. One who seeks constant improvement and is defined by their own path. The Brand Master utilizes available tools to evaluate the business and create a brand destiny based upon the brand's essence, objectives, and goals. Mistakes are part of the process, that's how lessons are learned. What's most important is that they become fewer and less costly. Decisions should be shaped by use of the appropriate navigation tools, such as THE BEAUTY BREAKTHROUGH THEOREM™ *(BBT™)*, defined in Chapter 1. The *BBT™* assesses brand stage, product cycle and consumer choices to determine next steps and brand fit.

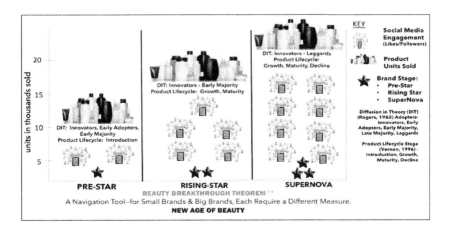

These factors should be included in the overall marketing year plan as well as incremental branding decisions. Brand Masters set plans in motion with: confidence in *Brand Essence*, knowledge of a solid *Culturally Cued Research* Analysis, *Niche Audience*, understanding of *Comprehensive Competitive Placement* (by price and position) and a strong *Integrated Marketing and Communication* Campaigns. All of which are necessary in launching a new product or refreshing an existing one, with a fully integrated Marketing and Communication Annual Campaign.

The goal of a marketing and communication campaign is to increase awareness for a specific product or service for a limited duration of time. Annual campaigns provide horizontal growth by enriching brand loyalty amongst existing consumers. Coupled with vertical growth—where a developing niche of new consumers are introduced by you or converted to your brand by a competitor—further expansion occurs. Brand Masters use all available tools to help determine their next steps.

WHO COMES FIRST?

THE CONSUMER OR THE BRAND?

Brand Essence
Consumers have the ability to mentally archive and categorize things—like favored products and services. They compartmentalize "go-to" products, those they like and those they love. In 2014, Media Dynamics, Inc. reported the average number of advertisements and brand exposures per day per person is well over 5,000. This included daily advertisement exposure from: television, digital streaming (Hulu), street- side, bus, train, cab, billboard, movie theatres, internet, and social media.

In a utopic world, brands develop Brand Essence and then market to consumers based upon the product or service. However, few brands have the time, resources, strategy or tactics to penetrate the vast amount of stimuli. Breaking through the clutter to develop a new category or sub-category requires deep resources and strategic planning. Tactics of enriched communication via messaging, advertising, social media penetration and niche consumer campaigns help to break through the excess and surface with successful innovation.

In mass, mainstream marketing, it's extremely challenging to create success in new categories of products or services. One reason is because mass categories have been in existence longer. The financial and labor resources are greater, and the technology for advancement is more extensive. Few brands have the time or resources to match that and create new categories with success.

Google, however, is a brand that has. They've created a successful new category initiated by search engines and expanding into internet related products and services. Google allowed the consumer to decide, over time, that this was a product/service they not only wanted, but needed. This was not without exceptional persistence, marketing, and heavy investment by Google.

Apple, another outstanding example of a brand leading by category, brand essence and efficacy versus consumer need. Apple tells consumers time and again, this is a product that you need. They first set a brand essence of fascination and uniqueness in the desktop and laptop specialty of design and utility. Aside from the genius in brand essence, positioning, price and message communication, Apple continues to launch line extensions in new categories, consistently telling consumers what they need: iPod in 2001, iTunes store in 2003, the iPhone in 2007, iPad in 2010 and the Apple Watch in 2015. This is rare. It doesn't happen often. Remember, only leading edge brands are able to create this type of innovation or have the resources to do so.

Sure, these are non-beauty examples, but they illustrate the volume of monetization that can be acquired when creation is supported by time, key messaging and resources.

In beauty, and specifically within Multi-Cultural beauty, categories have been dormant for decades. There's been very few new categories. In the past ten years, however, innovation in new subcategories has emerged — and with grand vigor from the new naturals movement.

CULTURALLY CUED

In A NEW AGE OF BEAUTY, the Multi-Cultural population explosion will absolutely propel technology and spur major innovation in Multi-Cultural beauty brands. General Market consumers (Caucasian, non-African American, non-Hispanic) are crossing over to peruse the Multi-Cultural aisles. African American/Hispanic consumers have always explored General Market aisles (relentless "right" product seekers). As the Multi-Cultural population explodes, the need for new categories and newer subcategories will continue. The beauty landscape will grow and flourish with expansion centered upon beauty needs and wants in hair texture, (melanin related) skin care, and products that multi-task (have multiple purposes).

The New Naturals Movement and the upsurge in styling products are leading by example. One of the tactics used in lieu of time and resource for products in new categories is emotion. No one *needs* a new beauty product. No one *needs* that new lip gloss. However, *want* gets transposed into *need* by emotion and value proposition.

If you're creating a new brand category or redefining an established category (or sub-category), it's important to know whether you're fulfilling a niche (or not) and if there's a slot for entry. Determine whether you're *making* a trend with the introduction or *following* a trend. Examine several dynamics — and consider the following:

- ➤ What's the emotional connection between the product and the consumer?
- ➤ How is emotion communicated?

> ➤ What value proposition does your brand promise to deliver?
> ➤ Who is your ideal client, new niche, or first group of consumers?

The truth is, it's very difficult to make a consumer compartmentalize a new preference for you. Creating a new space in the consumer's mind can be very challenging.

However, evoking emotion is a powerful communication tool and tactic. Evoking emotion as a brand to a consumer is like being in love. It supersedes logic, theory and tradition, and forms an attraction to your brand that lasts. A strong brand message with an emotional connection to the consumer has the power to create magic that translates into longevity.

SMART BRANDING

Brand: Carol's Daughter, www.bornandmade.com
Type: Mass
Products: Skin, Hair, Body
Brand Pillars: Natural, Authenticity, Real, Self-Confident

The #BornandMade Campaign has inspired thousands to be who they were born and made to be – not who others think they are "supposed" to be.

BRAND STORY + CREATIVE DESIGN

Tell your story. Stories connect people. It's a powerful tactic in marketing and communication.

Writer and social anthropologist, Zora Neale Hurston, created her classic novels based on folklore—stories of communities of people passed on through generations by word-of-mouth. Even in a digital NEW AGE OF BEAUTY, everyone loves a good *Brand Story* because it evokes emotion and inspires connection.

If you don't have a Brand Story, you're just another product or service. Brand Stories aren't just about being different, but it is a way to differentiate yourself from other brands. It's more than a slogan or catchy tagline. It's an opportunity to think beyond the functionality of the product or the service. Stories bridge brand loyalty and value. Great stories make people *feel something* — which is important, because emotions create powerful connections.

Your Brand Story is the root of your brand. It's the foundation that people can attach to, where they find something that resonates with them and what that they care about. As a business, it also and very importantly, offers something they want to buy into. When people bond with your brand, it creates brand loyalty.

SYNERGIZE THE CREATIVE

Another important element to remember is your Brand Story sets your brand tone, or narrative — which extends to *all of your creative* connecting points. Everything you touch, your brand colors, textures, packaging design, presentation, business cards, to the staff you hire, even your website design — is connected to your narrative. If your product is an ultra-premium luxury item with a high price point, but, your website looks as if it is first website, then there's a big disconnection between your brand essence, brand story and the visual or creative elements you express them with.

The visual creative is equally important in invoking brand emotions. All are a part of your story, your Brand Story. Every creative element reflects your Brand Essence, Brand Story and the truth you're telling the consumer (or potential consumer) about your brand.

BEAUTY INFLUENCER + THE BRAND STORY

As a Beauty Influencer, connecting with your audience in new ways is always beneficial. You can do this and create a lot of value in your campaigns with clients and audiences by leveraging your client's Brand Story. Whether you share their story through your blog, video log, in-person appearance or social media platform, it's up to you. But you can develop a fresh emotional connection between you and your audience, and your audience and a brand. The brand's power will *grow exponentially*. Sharing a Brand Story makes you a part of them, an extension of them, a brand authority, a true influencer.

As a hired Beauty Influencer or one working *pro bono*, your role is to have as much foresight about the brand as possible and to create connectivity points. The dots that resonate between your audience and the brand's audience are the connectivity points.

If your client hasn't provided a Brand Story, inquire about it. You weren't hired to create their marketing story, nor do you have enough information to do so, but asking will show them you're concerned about their position and that you care about the brand. It may prompt them to have their marketing and communications team create one.

Perhaps an equally important question: Do you have a Brand Story — as a Blogger or Influencer? And does your Brand Story mirror your brand image and brand promise?

One of the most common mistakes ever. I'd say 8.5 out of 10 beauty brands I have ever worked with make this same predictable and unnecessary mistake of creating too many skus, promoting either too many at once or not zoning in on the "hero" product or sku. Creating product after product without a strong brand essence, efficacy or marketing and communication campaign support will only increase your inventory. You may be able to push product to retail distributors, based on sales relationship. But, it will not pull product off shelf from consumers. Trying to be everything to everyone, is the antithesis of a Brand Master.

Check out Emily Weiss, her branding is doubly smart. A successful Beauty Blogger turned Beauty Brand and she really got the hero sku(s) delivery "right." Weiss started by interviewing real women about their beauty, very often on their bathroom floors.

SMART BRANDING

Brand: Glossier, created from blog – IntotheGloss.com
Type: Mass
Products: Minimal Beauty Products
Brand Pillars: Real women, real beauty, beauty routines of inspiring women

Blogger Turned Beauty Product Brand
You may know **Into The Gloss** — a blog created by **Emily Weiss** in her apartment with a notebook, a computer, and a passion for beauty. Armed with a camera, she set out to interview models, makeup artists, and strong women she admired to find out about the products they used and why. The blog quickly gained a worldwide following and Emily quit her day job. Today, **Into The Gloss** is a super successful resource and creative think-tank with a loyal, influential readership. It has a team with a keen sixth sense of what's relevant (and what works) when it comes to beauty: *"We've tried every product under the sun, interviewed many of our icons, and peeked inside hundreds of coveted beauty cabinets. You know we 'get it' because you 'get it.'"* Weiss' brand Glossier is a sensation with innovative products like the boy brow grooming pomade for eyebrows.

SMART BRANDING

Brand: @LipsticknCurlss, Jade Kendle,
www.lipstickncurlss.com
Type: Beauty Influencer
Product: Beauty Influencer for hair, skin, make-up and
recently as a toothpaste model for a Colgate
Optic commercial.
Brand Pillars: beautiful, ambitious, educated, aspirational
persona, real life, real beauty

Vlogger Turned Commercial Model, Actress + Ambassador
I've worked with Jade Kendle (@lipstickncurlss) with a variety
of brand campaigns. Not only does she have an amazing and
loyal consumer reach, she is one of the most professional beauty
influencers I have ever worked with. And I've worked with
dozens. Some other powerhouse Beauty Influencers I've
worked with include *@Sumetra Reed*, *@NaturallyTash*,
@Nae2Curly and the God Mother of Brown Blogging, *@Afrobella*
to name a few.

I speak of Jade because she has a unique Brand Essence as a
Vlogger, her style is distinctive. She curates fresh content for
brands that is unique to Vlogging. Jade is also prompt,
proactive, curious and anxious to go beyond the ask and be
create impactful brand campaigns. When I found out she was
cast in a Colgate Optic commercial, I wondered if she was cast as
a Beauty Influencer or model? She looks like one, and has the
panache to do both. We'll have to watch the commercial to find
out.

"People don't know what they want, until you show them."
-Steve Jobs

ATTRACT YOUR NICHE AUDIENCE

A mistake I've seen far too often with small and some large brands is wanting to be everything to everybody. It's just not possible. Brands do not have enough time or money to reach everyone, not to mention it's an ineffective longevity or growth tactic. In wanting to deliver to everyone, you're essentially diminishing the specialty of the brand. Having "everyone" as a target audience says the brand isn't specialized enough to cater to one or two uses or audiences.

Besides, if it's for everyone, it's no longer special. It doesn't speak to the consumer who has a real need or specific product want. When a brand decides who their tribe is, who their people are, and begins to research unique ways to attract them, it's at that moment that the brand will pivot for longevity and maturity.

In A NEW AGE OF BEAUTY, in the endless world of digital, the audience as a beauty brand is as much the Consumer Audience as it is the Beauty Influencer. The Beauty Influencers are primarily early adopters (Rogers, Diffusion of Innovation Theory,1962) by nature of being a beauty Blogger/Vlogger. Early adopters have been the word- of-mouth heroes for many successful brands. They get to seek and share what's new now, first. Marketers and the mass market need Influencers — for exposure and validation. Using Beauty Influencers is a win/win!

JUST "LIKE ME" CONSUMERS

As a Marketer you want to find your niche audience of influencers, "*your tribe*," those who align best with your brand. Your niche audience are the people who say to one another, "You're like me." (Hanna & Meltzoff, 1993). We have a likeness and tend to imitate one another. The "just like me" archetypes of your brand create a tribe of similar behaviors. Lululemon Athletica does an excellent job of targeting women who wear tights, love heat and do yoga— just like one another. A brand's Target Audience should be a group of people who you create products for because their patterns, behaviors and lifestyles are similar. As a Brand Master, with a small tribe of loyal customers, they should miss you if your brand disappeared. Your brand should be so rooted within the consumer (and niche community) that they'd miss you if you're gone.

COMPETITIVE PLACEMENT - THE MARKETING MIX

Product, Placement, Promotion, and Price are the four P's of the marketing mix dynamic used by Marketers Internationally. The 4P's are the essential components that work together collectively in establishing a brand's unique selling proposition. Since the 4Ps were introduced in 1960 by Jerome McCarthy, the model has been extended to include the 5Ps 6Ps, 7Ps, 12Ps and the 15Ps, not to mention C and E model extensions and advancements. A partial list of the additions includes: People, Profit, Public opinion, Political Power, Process, Physical environment, Plan and Performance, to name a few.

Most marketers have used the Competitive XY Graph in their career. The standard XY graph differentiates your company from competitors, and sectors it by cost versus performance. The Competitive XY Graph was advanced by the Price-Benefit Map to set brand value (D'Aveni), The Strategic Control Map (McKinsey), Three (3) Generic Strategies of Competing (Porter): Job to Be Done—creating new markets from consumer need, Disruptive Innovative Strategy—innovation to break order and create new order (Christensen), and *Blue Ocean Strategy*— for differentiation and low cost to open up a new market space and create new demand (Kim and Mauborgne); and the Trade-Off Map, customer experience map (Rod, 2013).

The concepts above are tools to help navigate your brand to determine:

1. *Market Segmentation*
2. *Brand Value Proposition*
3. *Competitive Analysis – Brand Benchmarking*
4. *Pricing*

TACTICS TO PLACE COMPETITIVE PLACEMENT

It doesn't matter how you get there. What's most important is that your brand does the exercise to understand competitive placement in the marketplace. This will support where you live and how you navigate. I recommend using the classic Competitive XY Graph with an overlay of a new competitive analysis, the Petal Diagram. (Blanks, 2013). I like the Petal Diagram because it's a new way to look at competitors. It includes start-up considerations and companies in the competitive landscape, creating new market categories. This is especially effective for Multi-Cultural beauty brands. Start-up entry-to-market, or brands entering with new categories, are not relevant in the XY Competitive Graph. THE BEAUTY BREAKTHROUGH THEOREM™ (BBT™) can be utilized as an excellent layered approach and sub-segment of a start-up's entry using the Pre-Star or Rising Star (*refer to Chapter 1 for a breakdown of the BBT™ archetypes*).

Utilizing comprehensive tactics in assessing competitive placement upon entry to market and/or a new category is vital. The BBT® overlay assesses competitors that are within the same brand stage, as well as brands that are more advanced, to determine brand performance and potential performance. The Petal Diagram is also a great visual aid for investors to illustrate a brand's starting position, growth opportunities, sources of future customers and potential competitors.

Competitive Analysis provides data to determine a variety of factors for competitive placement. If you can comprehensively answer the following questions, you're on the right track to competitive placement, accuracy, and success:

1. *Who are your direct and indirect competitors?*
2. *Why would you win against the main competitors?*
3. *How would you win against the main competitors?*

When it comes to pricing, quality dictates. It's easy to low-ball the price to support entry into the market.

However, with a quality product, you win by pricing your product high. The best fruit is at the top of the tree, not the bottom. Provided, the higher price is supported by a quality product, strong positioning and distribution that aligns. The Petal Diagram breaks the competitive analysis down by market segmentation, brand value proposition, competitive analysis and pricing.

One of the most damaging and costly errors I've seen with almost every beauty brand I've worked for or with — the launch of new brands — just because. New brands should be launched because of a need for a new category or you are fulfilling a need for the consumer. Too often brands are launched recklessly, with poor or no strategic planning and left to survive on their own. Not to mention the cost of the launch including retail planogram requests for presentation, and the unsold inventory that will remain in the warehouse.

The early stage of evaluation and assessment is an ideal time to perform a Life Value Analysis, a requirement for any brand. LifeTime Value (LTV) is used to answer the question of how much a Customer Relationship Management (CRM) marketer can afford to spend to acquire a new customer — and still make money. This is the most basic analysis to be performed on your customers. In order to undertake this study, you need to know (or have a reasonable estimate of) how long a new customer will remain with you, what purchase behavior this new customer will have over the lifetime of the relationship and what the margins of the business are. LTV can be performed on the customer base as a whole or it can be used for segmenting customers.

INTEGRATED MARKETING CAMPAIGN (IMC)

The Annual Marketing and Communication Budget is a subset of the Profit & Loss (P&L) Statement. A P&L is a financial statement that reviews the revenue, costs and expenses incurred within a fiscal quarter or year. Every effective company produces a P&L, usually prepared by an experienced Marketing Executive and often produced in teams. Each company includes different factors with varying degrees of detail and complexity. Essentially, a P&L is a deduction in the cost of goods sold, expense from sales revenue, and a reported *gross margin*, also termed gross profit.

Before an Integrated Marketing and Communication campaign (IMC) can be developed, a budget should be prepared. This is usually done by the Branding Manager who's executing the campaign. It all starts with the budget and should include the estimated projection of costs, including the Cost of Goods (COG) required (Investopedia) to promote the campaign. Cost of goods is the cost of every item related to the product—the cap, seal, bottle, carton, fill, or other. Too often COGS are not properly assessed. Particularly with small start-ups, I've seen too many brands to count, develop incremental plans and off the cuff programs without a budget. Promotional plans that included sampling or trial of product without including the cost of samples.

Q: *How can you know whether you're overspending or enjoying a healthy cash flow?*

It all starts with your budget and Profit & Loss Statements budgets or create Profit & Loss Statements. However, mastery of the budget and P&L statements are crucial elements to the success of any Intra- or Entre-preneur.

Once the budget and P&L are finalized, integrated marketing campaigns can be developed. What is a marketing campaign anyway? It's a strategic marketing plan with a series of tactics from the marketing mix that may include product promotion through traditional or nontraditional tactics (University of Oregon, 2013) Traditional tactics include television, radio, print and word-of-mouth. Nontraditional tactics include digital/online, and guerilla marketing (apps, QR, experiential events, etc.). In the highly competitive industry of beauty— Multi-Cultural beauty, frequent campaigns are necessary. The goal of any campaign is awareness on varied levels, and sales.

The campaign is termed an "integrated campaign" because a mixture of promotional methods are woven together to reinforce one another. Today, the mixture of options is robust and chock full of varied promotional strategies to include digital.

MASTER BEAUTY INFLUENCERS

As a Beauty Influencer, you too, are a beauty brand owner. Although you're providing a service, your name and that service are your brand. While some of the marketing and communication tactics may not be directly related to your current business as an Influencer, understanding how your client operates is a powerful leveraging tool.

ATTN: Beauty Influencers and Brand Masters

Master your *Brand Essence*, know your *Niche (and sub-*

*segmented) **Audience**,* and be able to identify your main
Bloggger/Vlogger Competitors.

All Beauty Influencers are NOT the same. Once you've
defined your Blogger/Vlogger style, your forte and point of
difference (included in your brand essence), defining your
competitive placement will be much less complicated. As a
Beauty Influencer (Blogger/Vlogger), you're the middle
(wo)man, liaising between B2B and B2C business. It's a fine and
important line that requires trust and credibility from both
sides.

As you're building your annual budget or projected profits,
work to build long lasting relationships with brands. I
encourage beauty brands to develop annual campaigns that
include two to three Bloggers, maximum. Bloggers should serve
as Brand Ambassadors versus quick fix sales bursts.

Unfortunately, beauty brands play a large role in
encouraging Blogger promiscuity — bloggers jumping from one
brand to another with little to no interest or loyalty to brands
other than payment. When brands leverage Bloggers for short
quick-fixes, they subject the Beauty Industry to Blogger
promiscuity as a means to not just monetize their service, but
basic survival (particularly if the Beauty Influencer has chosen
this field as a full-time career).

The ability to become proficient, think independently, and
remain proactive versus reactive in a marketplace filled with
"me too" products and tactics — is an art in brand building at
the mastery level. The ability to make self-governing decisions
about your brand while conscious of competitors, but not lead
by their moves, while maintaining relevance, accompanies self-
confidence and a great deal of risk. Yet, the rewards are
exceedingly beneficial. I highly encourage you to become a
Beauty Brand Master.

PART II

ENGAGE WITH SMART BEAUTY BRANDING

5 ISYNERGIZE + MEASURE

"It's About Instant Gratification."
~Josh Bernoff

Are you integrating digital marketing and communication strategies in your campaigns? If you aren't? Then you should re-evaluate your relationship with digital? Online and social media platforms aren't passing fads. Social media isn't just for kids and email marketing does generate sales. Underestimating the power of digital in A NEW AGE OF BEAUTY, it's like market share left on the table. The dream of becoming a SuperNova brand

Deferred by ignoring the power of digital, social media and Beauty Influencers.. (Brand Matrix, Beauty Breakthrough Theorem™, Taylor, 2016).

FROM LOCAL TO GLOBAL

There are 2 billion active social media users worldwide. (We Are Social, 2015) Marketers now have the opportunity to reach the masses on a global scale — simply by a click of a button. The ability to impact an extraordinary amount of people like *never* before is happening *now*. In 2015, social media was 9.9% of marketing budgets, by 2020 in just four short years that percentage is expected to double, to 22%. (HubSpot, 2015)

As a Brand Manager for Johnson Products in the early 2000's, social media didn't exist and digital advertising was too new to have solid metrics. Less than a decade later companies like Carol's Daughter had entire departments to leverage their inbound marketing. Social media drives traffic to websites, 31.24% of the time. (Shareaholic, 2015)

The traditional Beauty shopping experience is done by smelling the perfume, trying on the lip gloss and matching the concealer or foundation. However, in a digital world, the NEW AGE OF BEAUTY, shopping is done virtually. Strong visuals, great brand stories and "smart copy" rule the content. Although, what digital lacks in interfacing, it makes up for in visuals. Illustrative photos and demonstrative videos rewrite the shopper's experience, for a new way to encounter beauty.

CONTENT IS KING — WITHIN INBOUND MARKETING

Inbound marketing is **modern-day marketing, influenced by digital.** Digital is the tactical tool to breed success in **A NEW AGE OF BEAUTY**. The traditional marketing rules are broken and InBound Marketing is now King. The shopping behavior of your consumer has changed, and the methods for garnering their attention have changed as well. In order for beauty brands to attract customers, marketers have to provide them with content they want — content they love and content they want more of.

InBound Marketing is a holistic, data-driven approach to marketing that attracts individuals to your brand and converts them into lasting customers. (HubSpot, 2015) Inbound is different because it employs search engine optimization (SEO's), blogging, attraction and keeps the customer centric. Instead of relying on traditional marketing which focuses more on pushing messages out, things like buying ads, buying email lists, sending direct mail, cold calling, SPAM emails, interruptive advertising and it keeps the focus on the marketer.

iSYNERGIZED CAMPAIGNS

Tools and tactics employed by InBound Marketing include content that draws the consumer to your website—blogs, interactive tools, photos/infographics, videos, presentations and reports. Content that attracts the consumer to you, versus Outbound Marketing, where you go to the target audience, dump or deliver your message and often disrupt the consumer in their flow.

INBOUND MARKETING TACTICS

Connecting with the consumer where they are live and breathe and in the channel they want to interact with you in, is key. Tactics include *Curated Content, Calls-to-Action, Lead Generated Segmentation* and *InBound Analytics*—four key tactics to successful InBound Marketing.

> ➤ *Curated Content*—Social Media, Blog, Websites, Call-to-Action, Keyword Search and Marketing Automation are great leveraging tools. Beauty Influencers already know that one of the easiest ways to attract consumers to you is through curated blog or vlog content, SEO the blog/vlog content , then promote it on social media websites.

> ➤ *Call-to-Action* through your website with offerings such as contest, surveys, newsletters, special opportunities via the landing page on your website. Consumers complete forms to get what you are offering.

> ➤ *Lead Generated Segmentation* – Create segmented email lists with automated emails using email marketing software like Mail Chimp or Constant Contact. These emails will guide the consumer towards your purchasing path.

> *Analyze, Analyze, Analyze* — Marketing campaigns with pre-determined metrics to determine which areas need optimizations for success.

There is a significance to inbound marketing that speaks directly to the bottom line. InBound marketing has an average acquisition costs is $135, whereas outbound averages $346 (HubSpot, 2012). InBound marketing acquisition costs are less because the channels are less expensive to engage in, versus traditional TV, print, radio and outdoor. It is the cost, plus the interest in digital engagement that attributes to the success of Inbound Marketing.

However, the major corporations are utilizing these lean tactics as well — because they are inexpensive, but primarily because they work.

WHAT IS DIGTIAL vs. SOCIAL MEDIA?

Social media is content curated sharing tools to participate on social networking. Web-based communication tools that allow people to engage with each other by both sharing and consuming information. The term 'social media' is used loosely these days, often to describe what we post to Facebook, Twitter, Instagram or Snapchat, Periscope and Pinterest to name a few. However, the 'social' in social media refers to engaging with other people by sharing information with them and receiving information from them. The 'media' in social media refers to a tool or vehicle, like the internet, unlike traditional media — TV, radio, newspaper. Combine the two and we create engaging community channels.

While it is important to distinguish social sites, from service sites and product sites. Digital is the format that social media hosts or lives on. Your website is digital. Social media is an integration of digital. All of the sties below are social media sites in the hemisphere of digital.

- ➤ Social media standard-bearers such as Facebook, Twitter, and Snapchat.
- ➤ Social services like Netflix, Paypal and Evernote
- ➤ Social support products to include Apple and Amazon.

WHICH SOCIAL MEDIA PLATFORMS?

Some Brands that are committed to being on every social media platform simply because it exists, or because it's "new" or "hot" — and aren't concerned about consumer segmentation or Brand Essence, not to mention Brand Mastery. We discussed this in earlier chapters. New social platforms launch yearly and more are in development as we speak. All aim to become as successful as Facebook and Twitter, but some are advancing simply with innovation. New services that attract consumers and align with their wants and needs.

In addition to new social sites, it is important to select social platforms that align with your beauty Brand Essence *and* with the resources, a social media manager, available manage the selected social sites with compelling content and consistency.

Here is a snapshot of the **Top 20 Social Media Sites of All Time** (*As of February 2016 — Reporting from Sept 2015 – Feb 2016*)

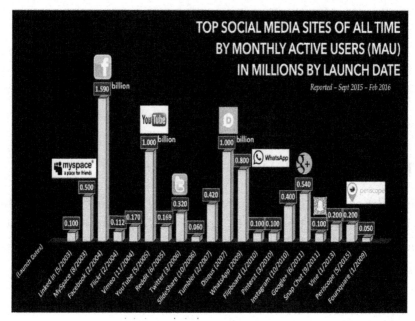

Sources: (LinkedIn, 2016) (ExpandedRamblings, 2016) (Through Feb 2016)

TOP 20 SOCIAL SITES INSIGHTS

A significant takeaway from the top 20 sites and recurring element is video. Video is a major component of 9 of the 20 top social sites of all time. More and more social sites are upgrading to in-line buy buttons. Consumers can purchase beauty brands and never leave their feeds on sites like Twitter, Facebook and Instagram. More in-line buying buttons, where consumers can purchase and never leave their feeds.

> ➤ *MySpace* – This is the social networking site that put the concept of social networking on the map, the "OG" of social networking. Surprisingly it's still alive. It's been nearly a decade since News Corp acquired the company for $580 million and roughly three and a half years since the media company sold the fading

property for $35 million to the Internet ad company Specific Media. ((Wall Street Journal, 2015)

➤ *Periscope* – A Twitter owned app and the fastest growing social media platform of 2015, with 200 Million streams in the first year. People are using Periscope for live events and to report events that occur around the world, like Baltimore uprising and the Nepal earthquake.

➤ *Meerkat* – Launched in March 2015, the site boasts 2 Million registered users. Though reporting sites like App Annie and Google Trends report shadowing numbers. The name, Meerkat, an animal that is very alert. The concept is people need to feel spontaneous together. Live Stream Your life, "live" and friends can watch simultaneously. (VentureBeat, 2015)

  o The live video market is getting crowded with introduction of Facebook Live and YouTube connect.

➤ *SnapChat* – A popular fun messaging mobile app that allows you to send videos and pictures, both of which will self-destruct after a few seconds of a person viewing them. You can take a photo or a video with it, then add a caption or doodle or lens graphic over top, and send it to a friend. Alternatively, you can add it to your "story", a 24-hour collection of your photos and videos, which you broadcast to the world or just your followers.

➤ *Disquis* - A blog comment hosting service for web sites and online communities that uses a networked platform. A "site to watch" great for content curators and publishers.

BEAUTY BRANDS IN A NEW AGE OF BEAUTY

The Digital Age has created a paradigm shift in modern beauty marketing and communication. Digital marketing has transformed the way brands allocate their marketing budgets. And, so it comes down to where to invest — digital focus plus talent teams, with brand niche categories (hair texture, skin hues) with multi-benefit products (innovation). Digital strategies must be implemented to intermix with a core role, not an ancillary position in communication campaign. Research shows that Inbound Marketing influences 70% of online sales. (*In Cosmetics*, 2015)

YOU MUST KNOW WHAT DRIVES CONSUMERS

Knowing what drives consumer behavior is the key to online sales success. Key steps to strategic BEAUTY brand building in the digital landscape.

1. Analysis – Brand engagement with consumers
2. Customization – Virtual "Try On" – Digital Solutions
3. Audience Focused – Retail Service Oriented
4. Compete – Comparability

THE MULTI-CULTURAL WOMAN + SOCIAL MEDIA?

The Multi-Cultural woman is a vital target audience in the NEW AGE OF BEAUTY. In the U.S. African Americans and Multi-Cultural women use their mobile phones more than their General Market counterparts.

Smartphone penetration levels are much higher for Blacks at 83%, compared to non-Hispanic Whites (75%) and the total population (78%). African-Americans use the Internet more across many topics, including entertainment, sports, dating, personal advancement and commerce. Black households with incomes between $75,000 and $100,000 are particularly active online. (Nielson, 2015, The Untold Story)

The Multi-Cultural consumer is a savvy social media enthusiasts, she uses more social media platforms than her counterparts. She is a loyalist and invests in many products, seeking the "right" beauty brand.

METRICS TO MEASURE SUCCESS

As a Beauty Influencer that wishes to create long-lasting relationships, and curtail brand hopping or Blogger promiscuity, developing success metrics is vital. It's important to work with the brand to develop mutually agreed success metrics in advance to ensure everyone is working towards the same goal. Success metrics encourage accountability from the brand and Beauty Influencer. A popular call-to-action tactic is customized discount codes for the Beauty influencer to provide in social media posts or videos. Although this tactic works, assuming every campaign will offer a discount to the consumer will lessen the campaign and brand value. Custom discount codes are effective, but not a tactic I would encourage for every campaign.

Enrolling the brand to optimize analytics to track campaign performance provides a stronger and more accurate testing measure of campaign effectiveness.

WHERE SHOULD I START MEASURING?

With so much to measure, it can be overwhelming to know where to begin. But, you must know how the consumer moves on your site to know what to test and to change. In doing so, here is a short list to measure against:

➢ How & Where? Track SEO, social media, blog, email, email segmentation, landing page, calls-to-action and automation in marketing.

➢ Segmentation is Key – Get custom reporting to under how different segments react to different campaigns.

➢ Contributors + Conversions – Understand the pages, content and sources of sales

METRICS THAT GET TOP BLOGGERS PAID

Top blog sites are paid a variety of ways that ensure accurate metrics. Those success metrics include:

Pay Per Click – A digital business model where a company that has placed an advertisement on a website pays a sum of money to the host website when a user clicks on to the advertisement.

- Top Site: HuffingtonPost, Ariana Huffington - $29, 896 Daily Income, a Value of $21.82M

Advertising - Banners, CPM, Private— Online **advertising** entails embedding an **advertisement** into a web page. It is intended to attract traffic to a website by linking to the website of the advertiser. CPM is cost per thousand impressions.

- Top Site: Mashable, Pete Cashmore - $15,781 Daily Income, a value of $11.52 Million

Affiliate Sales - As the business driving an affiliate program, you'll pay your affiliates a commission fee for every lead or sale they drive to your website.

- Top Site: WP Beginner, Syed Balkhi, $692 Daily

Income, a value of $505, 420

(Matt Smith, 2015) NOTE: *The website's featured in this **top 50 list** are estimates by Matt Smith, founder and editor of onlineteacher.com. The information is directional data used SiteWorthChecher.com, a free tool used to estimate the worth of a website.*

In **A NEW AGE OF BEAUTY** brands should intermix content strategy, promotion, and consumer interests in order to attract more relevant prospects and exceed campaign goals. To exceed goals, a brand must establish what the goals are which is where qualitative and quantitative success metrics, or key performance indicators (KPIs) should be formed. KPIs are the metrics that define success that are established by campaign members (Brands and Beauty Influencers) to lay out what success is. KPIs are a way managing expectations and keeping everyone clear on the goal.

And for Brand Executives, tools that manage social media posts and have embedded analytics like Buffer or Hootsuite, the analytics become easier to see and read through.

BEAUTY APPS

In our fast paced society, instant gratification is key. Consumers are more and more mobile in their daily lives and smart phones will incur the big advancements to accommodate for mobile and ever- evolving lifestyle.

The pursuit of beauty is directly connected to the digital mobile experience.

Science of email marketing reported that 80.8% of people read their email daily on their smart phones. More and more people are using smart phones to read their email daily.

A popular tactic in the 2000's were Quick Response codes,

known as QR codes. The single largest advancement in the beauty/smartphone relationship since smart phones were conceived. The largest advancement in beauty since smartphones were conceived. In the mid 2000's QR codes became popular and advertisers used them for adverts — everything from magazine ads to t-shirts.

QR codes were quickly advanced by mobile apps and the most recent Augmented Reality (AR) codes. Augmented Reality mobile apps allow you interact in real time with exciting digital content captured from all kinds of printed or physical objects and offers a multimedia library that can be experienced online and offline, anytime and anywhere.

> *L'Oreal* introduced the Makeup Genius in 2014. An AR mobile application that allows the consumer to try before buying. The app now boasts nearly 20 million users around the globe. L'Oreal is in currently in development of a new way expand the app. (QR Code Press, 2016) (Feb 2016)
> *Sephora* - Go App – Augmented Reality
>> o An array of augmented reality videos that play on a Sephora app on your smartphone. The videos show female founders of numerous cosmetic brands, such as Laura Mercier and Kat Von D, show-and- telling why their products are so special. Continue and these augmented reality background videos will pop up strategically throughout.
> New make-up application app, the Pocket Contour app. Snap a selfie and the app figures out what your face shape is (mine is round), then shows you exactly how to apply highlighting and shading makeup on your own face to create optical illusions that can define your cheekbones or hide a double chin. The app

also leads you to right shade of makeup to buy, at Sephora of course.

- o Beacons a third digital unveiling for 2016. The app provides special promotions, birthday month benefits, and get a reminded to take advantage of in- store services like mini-makeovers. (USA Today, 2015).

The tribe of Beauty Bloggers and Vloggers are key players in the authenticity and growth of beauty brands. Beauty and digital technology are a power couple. We are a selfie-obsessed society, driven by product comparison, price and peer reviews.

Beauty consumers can shop anywhere and anytime, and the number one method to research beauty is on a smartphone.

The future of beauty is rooted in video and mobile technology, a critical omni-channel success strategy

6 SEEK BFF'S

Sitting at the lunch table alone may make you feel lonely. So might playing on the playground solo. As an adult, similar conditions present themselves in business as well.

Succeeding as an entrepreneur requires a certain willingness to take risks. Many times that includes going it alone to do something new, different, something you've never done before—something a great deal of your family and friends may not understand. The passion and spirit of the lonely entrepreneur's journey is to be commended. Nevertheless, some of the most sustainable endurance brands have startup success stories of partnership.

As consumers we create preferences, an affinity toward specific beauty brand products we like most, that work for our needs. We're attracted to beauty brands with convenience, image, price, brand reputation and other factors that support our lifestyle and economic influences. Much can be said about the brands we gravitate to, the brands we trust and rely upon to deliver promised benefits. When a brand delivers, we want more. As consumers, we're open to experiencing new brand extensions, new opportunities from the companies we herald loyalty to. This openness is where partnership brand marketing begins. When companies unite, it creates value. Value enriches benefit and offers combined assets to drive growth further.

WHAT TO EXPECT FROM HEALTHY PARTNERSHIPS

Marketing and Communication Brand Partnerships are most successful when brand characteristics intersect with value, style and mission parallels.

The most critical component of the partnership is that both brands have built-in audiences. The audiences can be different but should have similar lifestyles, emotional cues and user experiences. The targets should be the same as this is where the new consumers will be leveraged by having different audiences amongst brands. When two potential brand partners have different target demographics, it sweetens the pot. By engaging with a new audience, both partners will most likely garner new customers, and ultimately, new sales growth.

STEPS TO DEVELOPING HEALTHY PARTNERSHIPS

It's important to know what you're working with before joining forces. Consider the following:

> ➤ Honesty Wins. Be honest about the scope and the deliverables of your company. No one wants to work with dishonest people who can't deliver.

> ➤ Define what success looks like in advance. Using Key Performance Indicators (KPIs), consider the qualitative and quantitative success metrics of the partnership campaign.

> ➤ Create a legal agreement for the partnership — with built-in separation stipulations. Partners often do not prepare for how the shared assets will be split upon separation. Agreements help define roles, responsibilities, risks, rewards, payments, including in the event of separation. All things end eventually. Few firms have the same partners for 25 years. Agreements also help keep brands

out of court. An excellent and highly recommended Marketing & Communication Attorney is Nakia Gray, Esq. (NakiaGray.com). She's as leading-edge as they come with a digital legal firm, based out of Washington, D.C.

➢ Co-create the Timeline and Business Plan. Establish every step of the When, How, and with What, so communication and deliverables run smoothly and according to plan.

> *"One Woman Can Make a Difference –*
> *But Together We Can Rock the World!"*
> **~Unknown**

SUCCESSFUL PARTNERSHIPS GENERATE GROWTH

Two is greater than one (most of the time anyway). Understand the benefits that can be obtained through partnership.

Qualitative (quality) growth. This occurs when the value in composition or character increases. Greater differentiation from competitors and increased niche offerings can result— as well as enhanced perception by consumers. Consumer attitude toward the brand is nourished and strengthened by the partnership.

Quantitative (#) Often brands are able to acquire the other partner's distribution channel. This is an invaluable asset from the partnership, minus the time and logistics for placement (e-commerce or shelf). The ultimate goal in Quantitative growth is increased awareness and sales.

BRAND MATRIX

Within the Brand Matrix of THE BEAUTY BREAKTHROUGH

THEOREM ™, partnerships offer advantage throughout all three brand stages: Pre-Star, Rising Star and SuperNova.

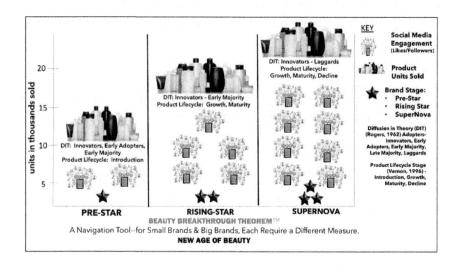

A Pre-Star, a fresh new brand emerging into the beauty landscape, could see exponential growth through partnership. A young brand may not have the followers to exchange through partnership. This could limit the reach of the partnership to local collaborations versus regional, national or international exchanges.

Yet a Pre-Star with strong Brand Essence, spot-on messaging and fresh newness of innovation can offer diversity through a different Multi-Cultural audience with a plethora of digital offerings to connect in new ways.

Rising-Star and SuperNova brand stages are prime for partnerships as well. Having a reputation with consumers, partnering for unique campaigns with digital and with experiential events, can create strong consumer relationships. LIVE panel discussions, conferences and discussion type forums are popular methods that brands who are collaborating with one another are using to convene with consumers over conscious issues that matter to them. This is a powerful tactic that escapes the digital space and returns to human communication. I foresee this trend continuing, and integrating it with advanced technology, live at events.

SuperNova brands specifically can advance in the international arena through joint ventures. A SuperNova emerging onto the global scene is like a Pre-Star entering their native market place. Although as a SuperNova there's a familiarity in the native country, U.S. brands are in demand globally and often surface with ease without strategic distribution. Entering the beauty marketplace in a foreign environment with a strong brand partnership creates instant trust by brand association. This is why the exchange of loyal followers is so key. Both brands win when new customers are gained through the collaboration.

BEAUTY INFLUENCERS + BRAND PARTNERSHIPS

Let's face it, Beauty Influencer programs are big business — and growing. There are ways to help slow or eliminate Blogger + Brand promiscuity, with little passion or purpose. The first and most important detail is to partner with an Influencer (for Brands) or Brand (for Influencers) that are an authentic fit." Aligned by brand usage, style and personality, yet can create growth opportunities. Though, the growth opportunity is usually attributed to the difference, the pockets to reach new audiences. Beauty Influencers should stop shopping around from one brand to the next. Just as Brands need to commit and invest in longer term partnerships to analyze campaigns and allow the relationships to grow. Good relationships take time to mature. To mix up the campaigns, diversify the activity or tactics for Influencers to use. Build a core triad of Influencers and allow them to represent your brand with a long-term commitment, as you would with a Brand Ambassador campaign.

According to Nielsen Research (2015), 92% of consumers trust recommendations from other people — those they don't know — over content created by a brand. Selecting the right Beauty Influencer partnership is no different than joining forces with a corporate brand. Partnering with a Beauty Influencer is like partnering with a journalist, an award winning columnist whom people love, trust and follow. However, in the case of the Beauty Influencer, they're usually paid to promote a brand for a campaign.

Selecting a Blogger or Vlogger based solely upon sizeable social media followers is a mistake. I've worked with Bloggers and Blogger Management teams (yes, some Bloggers have management representatives — though I've never seen them last long) who were not the most prudent or professional — though their social media numbers were through the roof. Not to mention, some Influencers purchase "likes" and followers. *More on FTC social media enforcement in chapters to come.*

Research the Blogger or Vlogger of interest. This is an investment that should yield returns via: awareness, expanded consumer database and ultimately, monetization. Ask important questions and go slowly. Commit to a short term relationship with renewable options in writing. Beauty Influencers who are able to blog or vlog fulltime rely on their brand/brand business to support them. Leveraging longer term relationships and diversifying campaign usage are vital to creating healthy product brand to Beauty Influencer brand relationships. In the digital age of digital marketing, where so much business is done electronically, impart some human communication. Have an in-person conversation or a phone call with the Blogger, Vlogger or Influencer directly. Don't only communicate with their management or PR team, but meet or speak directly with them. Hear the enthusiasm (or lack thereof) from the Beauty Influencer first hand. Remember, this is the potential voice of your brand, at least for a specified time.

TACTICS FOR BRANDS + BEAUTY INFLUENCERS

> ➢ Product Seeding - Beauty Influencers are sent products for trial. It's important to add a personal touch and make it special, "just for them." This particular tactic works best with large, well-known, well-followed Influencers, to garner the highest impact. On the contrary, when sending out a product or gift to a Blogger, be sure you will gain something in exchange as a result of the brand seeding.

> ➢ In 2015 I seeded Afrobella with product from a client well known haircare brand in Naturals category. It was a new product and she was the first to receive it. Afrobella posted it because she genuinely liked the product. She found out a day or two later that she was the first to receive the product— and no other blogger had it, it hadn't even gone in retail distribution. She re-posted a second thank you. Fruit from the seed, for sure. A valuable post from the "God Mother of Brown Beauty Blogging," as she is endearingly referred to by the Beauty Industry. This was a valuable exchange. Afrobella.com

> ➢ Sponsored Posts - There's nothing wrong with admitting that you've paid an Influencer to post about your brand. And that's a good thing, because the Federal Trade Commission (FTC), the agency that enforces U.S. truth-in- advertising laws, has been reinforcing their Endorsement Guide ever since it was released in 2010. Bloggers should note on their social media posts when their story has been sponsored by a brand (opinions are their own) or simply title it, "Sponsored Ad." I don't

suspect infractions though, unless there's a large corporate brand involved.

> Sponsored Posts - A successfully sponsored post through Desk, a New Blogger App, was sponsored on John Gruber's blog. Soon after, the creators of Desk were inundated with requests from other prominent bloggers. The Result? Desk was awarded "Best App of 2014 and 2015" by Apple. This was a successful sponsored post.

> Product Reviews - Consumers research and seek product reviews before making purchase decisions. According to Hubspot, 84% of consumers research a brand, service or product before buying it.

> Influencer Takeover - An exciting way to introduce your audience to a fresh voice and garner new consumers by utilizing an Influencer's presence, through a "Beauty Influencer Takeover." The Beauty Influencer will take charge of the social media site for a day, or a weekend. It's a refreshing way to create new content and cross-promote new audiences.

> Contests, Giveaways and Group Giveaways. Impactful tactics create mass brand awareness and expand database and e-mailing lists to grow the business. Everyone knows what a contest and giveaway is. Essentially, a brand provides a prize from an exchange of data or action from a consumer. A group giveaway is when a brand enrolls 10 to 20 Influencers for simultaneous brand giveaways, all on the same day. This offer magnifies brand exposure versus a single giveaway from a single Blogger. If the contest is streamlined into one system, the brand team will save time and money. Bloggers also get added exposure by cross-promoting the group.

➢ Brand Sponsored Ad Space. An advertisement can be sponsored by a brand directly or by an Influencer — the brand has more control over the messaging this way.

➢ Collective Influencer Competitions. This tactic should be leveraged by Rising Star or SuperNova brands. Established brands would benefit most, whereas a large number of Bloggers would have brand recognition. Also, the brand should have a budget to support competition of this scale.

➢ Collective Influencer Competitions are competitions where Bloggers ask their followers to vote for them in a themed contest. Prizes could include: brand collaborations supported by print/digital press, Brand Ambassador or travel opportunity on behalf of the brand, and bragging rights for the year or term. This is an excellent tactic to reach a variety of Blogger audiences and collect an exponential amount of names for your database through the voting process.

➢ Video / Vlogger opportunities are up-trending strategies. Videos drive awareness, increase engagement, educate readers, inspire action, and are great for Search Engine Optimizers (SEO). In fact, 70% of the top 100 search listings on Google are video results. The social sharing of videos shift organic Google search results. A two or three second video can transmit emotion, history and education to deliver Brand Essence in a blink. Videos are also perfect for partnership programs because they're easy to share, are more engaging than static images, and have strong behavior analytics and SEO options.

SUPER SMART BRANDING

Brands: OPI (OPI.com) + Refinery 29.com
Type: Mass
Brand Pillar Connection: Fun, Colorful, Industry Leaders
(Wong, February)
Partnership

Brand
OPI, a leading nail polish company, + Refinery 29.com — a
fashion, style and beauty website.

Tactic
OPI created a video with cool mood evoking music to promote
a new nail polish color and style. The Half-Moon Mani, in mint
green. The Half-Moon Mani is essentially a French manicure
with a modern twist, inspired by Spring 2015 Fashion Week.

Result
The results of web traffic, CPM's (clicks per thousand or sales
for OPI, mint-green nail lacquer are undetermined, but the
video was great created brand excitement.

> ➢ Affiliate or Referral Programs. You can either join an
> established affiliate or create your own. Affiliate
> programs work in partnership with a Blogger who
> drives traffic to a product site. The product brand pays
> the Blogger a percentage of each referral, a mutually
> beneficial agreement. Most major retailers use an
> established affiliate program like ShopSense or
> LinkShare, based purely on volume.

> ➢ Beauty subscription boxes. This is an excellent way to get
> product reviews with an insert in a box to prompt digital
> review (provided the brand has enough samples in

inventory). Curls Understood, a leading subscription based beauty box goes a step further in their liaise positioning — brand (B2B) to consumer (B2C). Curls Understood offers a unique marketing mix: product promotion, customer feedback, hair data, dedicated digital content, dedicated email and digital advertising. Also, each beauty box subscriber completes a 1-minute survey to assess their hair (texture, porosity and density), demographics (race, age, location) and consumer product feedback (on the products used), to engage the subscriber with products that make sense. It also garners qualitative and quantitative data for clients (hair enthusiast consumers and beauty brand manufacturers.

➢ Beauty Influencer to Beauty influencer (B2B) partnerships are also a great way to organically leverage brand exposure, while bonding as women and entrepreneurs. There are many panel discussions, expositions and trade shows — predominantly around The Natural Hair Movement — but I believe an even more powerful force can manifest by forging Influencer to Influencer partnerships.

CORPORATE SOCIAL RESPONSIBILITY (CSR)

> *"When we give cheerfully and accept gratefully,*
> *everyone is blessed."*
> **~Maya Angelou**

In 2015, I wrote an article in OTC Beauty Magazine, a Multi-Cultural Trade Beauty Industry print publication entitled, *"A Call for the OTC Philanthropist!"* OTC's are the beauty supply stores in every urban neighborhood across the United States.

They're the Sally's Beauty Supply stores of the inner cities. OTC's dwell in areas that are playgrounds for renewal and rebuilding, aka: Urban America.

Within most cultures and societies throughout the world, the adage "With great power comes great responsibility," dictates morals and values. As an established fixture in a community where one's wealth is acquired, it becomes a social responsibility to contribute to the community that sustains the OTC business.

Developing a platform of social responsibility is a corporate, social and human responsibility that speaks volumes about your business. It says you care and it gives consumers a "reason to believe" and continue to support your business— and with more enthusiasm!

WOMEN create wealth for beauty and personal care companies in the U.S. Profits are estimated to reach $81 Billion by 2017.
(EuroMonitor Interantional, 2015)

1. **Karma Bank.** It's the right thing to do. Giving is a human, social and business responsibility.
2. **Long-Term Cause.** Support the people in need that support your business. Commit to a cause and develop a long-term strategy.
3. **Incite a Spirit of Giving.** Increase consumer and corporate staff respect and morale. Show that you stand for worthy values. Ask your staff to donate via time or cash donations.
4. **Action.** Show the women and the community you serve that you care about their needs and appreciate their support of your business.
5. **Increase Awareness.** Build awareness for a selected charity and connect it to your brand. Utilize public

relations to leverage partnerships and integrate into digital format.

6. **Tax Breaks.** Charitable contributions are tax deductible – 501(c)(3). Leverage them.

WHICH CHARITY SHOULD I PARTNER WITH?

Teaming up with a long-term philanthropic partner may seem like an overwhelming task, but if you reach from your Brand Essence, your ideal charity will surface. Identify customer patterns gained from Brand Research. Discover what their needs are. Then think about a common challenge this customer group has. People who need help are the easiest to find and offer endless opportunities to give a hand: health and weight concerns, domestic abuse, parenting skills, support of children, career development, educational opportunities—and the list goes on.

Lastly, use a search engine and the resolve options are infinite. Opportunities to align with existing causes and their programs make Corporate Social Responsibility easy.

SMART BRANDING *Partnerships*

I'm an advocate of discovering your charity of choice at the beginning of your business journey—at the onset of brand development, understanding it may change. Although as a Pre-Star, without investors, you may feel like the charity yourself! LOL.

Carrying a charity as you develop your brand is a noble and powerful tool for consumer perception. In the beginning, your contribution may include time and talent, building to include fundraising or other non-financial assets. In summary, whatever partnerships you're seeking, do the research. Ensure you're aligning with a partner who fills your voids, supports your weaknesses, can increase your audience and enhance your overall public perception for goodwill.

7 HAVE YOU BEEN CALLED?

"Logic will get you from A to B.
Imagination will take you everywhere."
*~Albert Einstein*Error! Bookmark not defined.

Einstein's quote explains what entrepreneurs intrinsically understand: logic creates boxes and limitations. It's the non-traditional, unorthodox, unconventional ideas that create change. Entrepreneurs are "the great change agents." They are the doers. They don't just want to change their lives; they want to change the world. By the nature of this lifestyle, of course there's the want to monetize opportunities—but most of all, it's to change the world and invoke more meaning into it. Otherwise, they could work for someone else and be comfortable with limitations.

It's said that ministers receive a call from God upon their life, for their work. An entrepreneur is said to have a similar spirit or calling. Steve Blanks, serial entrepreneur and USC Educator, describes it as "a calling that won't quit." It's a strong repetitive beckoning. A calling that keeps you up all night and wakes you up early in the morning, eager to work harder than ever and to never give up.

"The idea of creating something from nothing, has to be a thirst," says Blanks, "an insatiable quest. A craving that won't quit." The entrepreneur knows well—the magnetic, ceaseless attraction of the mission. Therefore, passion should lead the way to the creation of any beauty product or service, not money or anything else.

U.S. Women are responding to the call with great vigor.

Women owned businesses grew 1.5 times the national average in 2015. *(2015 State of Women-Owned Business Report)*

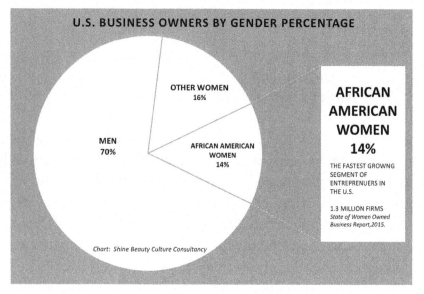

Source: 2015 State of Women-Owned Business Report, commissioned by American Express Open., Chart by Shine Beauty Culture Consultancy.

African American women are leading the trail, the fastest growing entrepreneurs in the U.S., owning 14% of all women-owned businesses, or 1.3 million businesses in total. African American women-owned businesses grew 322% since 1997.

Beauty Industry manufacturers are one of the strongest industries blazing those trails. The Natural Hair Movement has assisted in the amass of new African American brand owners. Year after year, thousands of new beauty brands emerge onto the scene. Manufacturers are enthusiastic about their products and what they might become in both U.S. and global market playing fields.

There are a host of reasons why people become Entrepreneurs. I choose to stretch into Entrepreneurship slowly, dabbling back and forth with freelancing until my confidence and strategic plan are strengthened. My creativity is unorthodox and my way of being fits better outside of the day-to-day corporate environment.

JUST WHAT IS AN INTRAPRENEUR?

An Intrapreneur is an "Inside Entrepreneur, an employee who's tasked by a company to make an idea or project into a profitable venture," according to Investopedia. The Intrapreneur has the spirit, passion and skill set of an Entrepreneur, yet backed with the resources and investment capital of a corporation. A significant challenge consistently faced by an Intrapreneur is to endure layers of corporate approval and internal politics. This tends to incite fear from a lack of job security. There are a plethora a reasons for internal politics but it usually stems from four categories: Leadership (or lack thereof), Corporate Culture, Organizational Issues, and Staffing & Communication Challenges (Society of Actuaries, 2005)

ARE ENTREPRENEURS BORN OR MADE?

My answer is both. It's the spirit of manifesting the idea into reality and success. The natural "Go-Getters" feel it coming from deep inside. These are the Born Entrepreneurs. And there are those who come from families of entrepreneurs. They've watched their families develop businesses their whole lives. Industrialist families like the Luster's (haircare brand from Chicago, Il), the Bronners (haircare and trade show Atlanta, Ga) and the Weingartens (Essie Weingarten, nail polish company, Queens, NY). Those who learn how to take control of their financial destiny by studying, watching, learning and listening to others are Made Entrepreneurs. Being an Entrepreneur inherent and the effort comes a little harder. Essentially, Made Entrepreneurs have to learn to think and operate.

If you don't like hard work, aren't comfortable adapting to

social norms and corporate guidelines, and most importantly, if you aren't able to ride the financial peaks and valleys of Entrepreneurship, it may not be for you.

There are many reasons people believe they can become successful Entrepreneurs. I agree that beauty business owners can be made as well. The industry is very specific, but most of the characteristics are malleable. Entrepreneurship can be cultivated through study, will, desire and passion.

"I did not have the most experience in the industry or the most money, but I cared the most."
~Sara Blakely, Spanx

PITCH WITH PASSION

Many will tell you that without passion, you have nothing. You can rehearse, re-write, and practice your pitch over and over. The reality is, without passion, your pitch, mission and efforts will resonate as insincere. Passion gives you confidence, it allows you to rely on yourself and trust your instincts. Passion gives you that invaluable internal spark.

PASSION FOR PURPOSE – OVER PROFIT

In my 15-year career in beauty and business, I've talked with countless Entrepreneurs. One common thread that rings true for 90 percent of them is that passion and purpose inspire them every day. It's challenging to rationalize working around the clock and missing holidays, special events, and precious moments with family and friends, to anything other than passion and purpose. It must be rooted in something bigger than you, a cause bigger than just money.

As an Adjunct Professor, I seek to enlighten my students by explaining to them that it's okay if they haven't figured out their purpose yet. Most people don't know what their purpose is. But it's *not* okay to *not* pursue your purpose— daily. I'm told that purpose is static, but our approach to it, is what evolves. Meaning our jobs and relationships, the things we spend the most time in, are a part of our purpose whether we understand that or not. As you mature and get closer to who you are, you get closer to your purpose. Diligently tracking your purpose so you can link it to your passion is important—and ultimately leads to monetizing profits.

For instance, if your big picture purpose is to unite and celebrate people from all walks of life, that may be your life's work as well. In just under 20 years, Sean Meenan has become a multi-successful Entrepreneur, Restaurateur, Investor, Philanthropist, and Environmentalist. His passion is people and bringing them together. He's used this mission mantra— passion, in all of his capital ventures. Meenan is founder of *Cafe Habana,* a family of restaurants serving Dominican/Cuban/Mexican food, and Brooklyn's *Cafe Outpost, a* solar powered restaurant. He's one of Etsy's original investors (the digital legend, e-commerce marketplace "where people around the world connect to sell and buy unique goods"). He's also co-founder and investor in *The Elder Statesmen*, a luxury apparel brand, celebrating the artisan discipline and the people behind it. As for philanthropic work, Meenan founded *Habana Works*, a weekend design program for parents and children. "For me, it was more about betting on the passion. Helping people realize their dreams is the best thing you can do." (Lopez, 2013)

Or, consider Beauty Industry veteran, Germaine Bolds-Leftridge, successful serial entrepreneur and long-time client. Leftridge is a Visionary. She supports women through industrialization and monetization. There's no better way to show someone you believe in them than to invest in them directly or position them to create their own legacy. *Germaine does both.*

I've learned so much watching her navigate the "Boy's Club" beauty business. She's a deep thinker. A Strategist. Deliberate in her staff selection (95% women, including beauty sales managers, merchandisers and beauty street teams), *"I don't waste time with people that don't have passion, or that I don't believe in."* Leftridge unapologetically affirms quite often.

She's a master at creating winning partnerships and helping to position women to build stronger legacies. Germaine has been a pivotal pillar of support and wisdom, both personally and professionally. She's makes it her purpose to support women to help them build stronger legacies—mainly because she knows women are the cornerstone of society. Germaine understands that as women, we have the power to create or destroy—and when we're empowered, we're unstoppable.

Leftridge employees over 200 women. She inspires, motivates and promotes them on their journey through her businesses: GBL Sales Inc., a sales firm of over 20 years headquartered in Columbia, Maryland; and Ubiquitous Expo (Est. 2014) a Hair, Health & Beauty Tradeshow, held at The Washington, D.C. Convention Center.

Passion lives within each of us. How we funnel it leads to our success. Passion will make you want to work harder than you ever have before, and never give up. The focus may evolve, but the passion remains constant. With practice, some failure, more practice, and a lot of heart— passion leads to profits.

8 GET RETAIL READY!

*"Content is King and Distribution is Queen...
and She Wears the Pants."*
~Jonathan Perelman

I've developed literally hundreds of winning presentations for Planogram Reviews—new product presentations ("decks or presentation decks" as we call them in marketing) where a retailer reviews a product and its marketing and communication strategies along with business projections, to determine whether a retail store will select the brand's product to place on the store's prime real estate—store shelves. The preferred position is a certain height on shelf, placed on an end-cap (an aisle position) or in a customized display. The process is very detailed with brand overview, point of difference, pricing and competitive landscape, etc. At renewal time, it may also include the potential for deciding to grow your business with greater distribution—more retail doors.

This may incite fear. There are many dynamics involved in distribution, beyond the fantasy and monetizing allures of having your brand in retail stores. There's the idea of growing too fast. Fear of the ability to maintain inventory, logistics, cash flow and overall operations is a common challenge and the pitfalls that occur with retail distribution.

If you're still producing your product in the kitchen or garage and haven't purchased or outsourced a manufacturing facility? Fear can grow by leaps and bounds—but don't let it. Trust the process. Implement smart inventory projections and marketing plans for an effective push through to retail and pull through to consumers.

COMMON THOUGHTS + CONSIDERATIONS

➢ *Will a manufacturer be able to make my product well?*
➢ *Will it come out the same?*
➢ *What about product stability?*
➢ *What if someone steals my formulation?*
➢ *Will I be able to pay for the manufacturing of my product through a manufacturing plant?*

These are legitimate concerns that can be addressed with reputable manufacturing houses. Sort out the manufacturing and get quality billing itemizations. Plant production facilities are in business to produce products.

Most manufacturers are willing to negotiate and create flexible agreements with unit commitments to support the cost of prodution. Reserving enough time to negotiate the best terms will pay off. Manufacturing is one of the keys to COG savings for beauty owners.

Out-of-stocks can ruin your reputation, create an absorbent amount of fees and damage your retail and consumer relationship.

WHEN TO SEEK NATIONAL RETAIL DISTRIBUTION

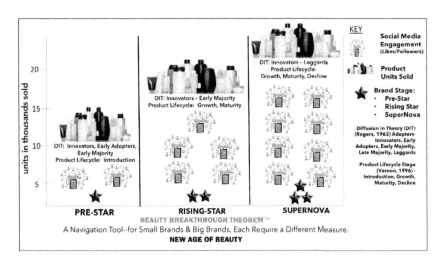

Most emerging brands today begin by selling their product on their brand e-commerce website. If you're in the Pre-Star stage of the Brand Matrix but approaching the Rising-Star phase, now is a good time to start exploring the process. A good rule of thumb: Start at least a year ahead of the time you want to be in retail. Planogram reviews are usually twice a year, Fall and Spring. Keep this in mind as you decide to connect with a retailer, using an experienced Beauty Sales team that can help you navigate the business of beauty. and garner the retail stores you want while on-boarding you into the U.S. and International business — GBL Sales Inc. is a leading firm to consider.

As a beauty manufacturer, most brand owners have dreamed of seeing their product on-shelf, at their favorite in-store retailer, and in the hands of consumers and celebrities. But today, in A NEW AGE OF BEAUTY, within the e-commerce beautyscape, a brand's dream can expand to transatlantic, well beyond U.S. borders with ease, to quickly have international distribution. One of the most attractive elements of A NEW AGE OF BEAUTY is the digital age — the ability to create global reach, with the aspiration of international beauty paradigm shifts.

Traditionally, the ability to touch/smell (trial) and garner shelf/counter product advice has been important considerations for consumers when purchasing beauty products. However, brands are creating provisions for more modern conversions—for the traditionalist who looks online but doesn't purchase (beauty products) online. Conversion tactics include robust email marketing—with segmentation and testing. But let us not forget our mainstay of distribution—brick and mortar retail stores. Many online stores such as as AMAZON, are creating brick and mortar boutique stores or alternative outreach.

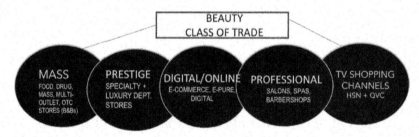

Figure 4 – BEAUTY CLASS OF TRADE, Chart & Design by Shine Beauty Culture Consultancy

BEAUTY INDUSTRY DISTRIBUTION

In-Store

- ➢ **MASS** - MULO - MultiOutlet, formerly FDM: which includes Food—Giant, Publix, Safeway, Wegmans, Rite Aid, Whole Foods Market, Trader Joe's, etc.
- ➢ Drug—CVS, Walgreens, Rite Aid, Target
- ➢ Mass, plus Walmart, Club and Dollar Stores (Family Dollar, Dollar General, Fred's).
  - o Beauty Supply Stores, known as B&Bs; account for at least 50% of the U.S. haircare business. This

class of trade does not have scanners to scan UPC codes and track purchases. And, so the sales are direct ship only, push through to the retailer, not pull-through to the consumer.

➢ **PRESTIGE** – Specialty/Department/Luxury—Macy's, Dillard's, Sephora, Nordstrom, Lord & Taylor, Barney's

Digital

➢ **E-COMMERCE** – The digital BeautyScape is multi-layered and expanding each year. *E-Commerce is one of the fastest growing beauty categories worldwide, with a global average of 57%* (Hana Ben-Shabat, 2015)

Digital Spaces:

1. Multi-Channel Retailers
   o Sephora (.com and brick + mortar)
2. Pure-E-Tailer
   o DooBop.com
3. Company Websites/Direct Sales
   o Amazon
4. Social Media Sites
   o Facebook, Twitter, Pinterest - Buy-In pages on social sites, so the consumer doesn't have to leave the site to purchase.
5. Mobile Apps
   o excerpts from digital pages translated to mobile.
6. In-Store Digital
   o Many stores are leaping into this multi-order area. Amazon has plans for a in-store with online options.
7. Beauty Box Subscribers / Auto-Replenishment Programs
   o CurlsUnderstood.com
   o CurlBox.com
   o BirchBox.com
   o PeriodBox.com
   o theHolBox.com

CONTENT + DISTRIBUTION

In A NEW AGE OF BEAUTY, the digital age of distribution, where aspirational branding drives long-term success, there's a human communication dynamic that's almost ironically driving digital success. It's the art of narrative and the ability to tell original and creative stories that are so vital to encouraging those aspirations. Online stores require a curator, a trusted brand ambassador leveraged for connectivity to the consumer, to create the elegant integration of content and commerce. Also to shorten the time between on-site engagement and transaction. Beauty brands and retail outlets are adapting as more consumers go online to buy beauty and personal care products.

Online sales represented approximately $4.3 billion of the overall (General Market and Multi-Cultural) beauty and personal care category, an estimated 6.5 % of the total category. (AT Kearney, 2014)

Sets, kits, skincare and make-up lead category purchases, while haircare, bath, shower and deodorants perhaps because of the lower spends that do not justify the shipping costs, unless combined with other items. A.T. Kearney's Analysis in Beauty and The E-Commerce Beast, 2014, substantiate the difference in segment spend: E-commerce penetration of 6% for mass and 11% for prestige [1] Prestige brands are the most successful online because the prestige price points are higher and the profit margins are better. Mass brands can reap benefits as well by coupling brands and kits together, for optimal profits.

Top 10 E-Commerce Sites for Buying Beauty & Personal Care

(A.T. Kearney, 2014) *The 15 websites were derived from a survey of 560 respondents who identified themselves as online beauty shoppers.*

1. Amazon.com	6. Macy's.com	11. Drugstore.com
2. Walmart.com	7. CVS.com	12. Beauty.com
3. Sephora.com	8. eBay.com	13. LOreal.com
4. Walgreen.com	9. Ulta.com	14. JCPenney.com
5. Target.com	10. Avon.com	15. Olay.com

SMART BRANDING

Specialty Online Beauty You Should Know

- DooBop.com– the first E-Tailer curated for the Multi-Cultural /Multi-Ethnic woman. Women with brown skin and textured hair. An online shopping destination, expertly curated by Jodie Patterson, Co- Founder.

- BeautyCounter.com– Their mission is to get safe products into the hands of everyone. A company devoted to environmental progress and health in beauty.

BEAUTY INFLUENCERS, BRANDS + RETAIL

Beauty Influencers haven't often been included in the retail discussion, but the time is now. Retail is an excellent opportunity for Influencer involvement with promotions. Campaigns that integrate blogging, social media and in-store or web guided promotions align seamlessly with the e-commerce business segment.

Another great opportunity to explore are holiday gift sets endorse by beauty brands. Perhaps, if you're influential enough, an agreement on a percentage of royalties could be made. Multi-Cultural retail space has long been used by spokespersons, but the idea of integrating opportunities in retail and digital has enormous potential (and growth) for both Brand and Beauty Influencers

9 KEEP IT FRESH

Your mind is not a cage. It's a garden and it requires cultivating.
–Libba Bray

When a brand releases a new product with copycat taglines and disclaimers that include "hot" "new," and "cool," it gives me cause to pause. Following category leaders to release more of the same products with the same efficacy and usage—is not innovation. There's nothing "hot," "cool" or innovative about being a "Miss Me Too." There's no mastery in developing more of the same. Nothing has been created or advanced by copying.

Innovation is about pushing the envelope further, challenging the status-quo, and stretching beyond defined boxes to create something new and fresh. Something like a fresh way to use a product, for a specific type of body, skin or hair type. Or, to create ease of usage, purpose or multi- purpose. How can the product marketplace be so closed and saturated by the "same" when the Multi-Cultural target audience is so open to trial of new products?

African American and Hispanic women over-index in their spending compared to Caucasian women. The Multi-Cultural woman is in continuous pursuit of beauty and "right" products. The frontier is wide open for claim by beauty brands that pursue innovation.

Brands that pursue niche customization, multi-purpose products, mobile technology, video integration offerings, and convenience will WIN. New products specially adapted to an ethnic group for skin tone customization perhaps? Or tailored by age: baby, children or the aging—anti-wrinkle serums or eye creams, perhaps? Brands that create advanced formulations, cutting-edge technology, superior efficiencies, are forward-thinking, with multi-purpose efficacies — will become the leaders and the most successful. Women want brands to make their lives easier and simpler. Multi-purpose brands are seen as significantly more valuable. Who doesn't want a CC cream with collagen and an SPF moisturizer? Products that advances in functionality and efficacy, yet make life simpler will yield top sales and consumer conversions.

THE DUALISTIC APPROACH

There is a dualistic approach to smart beauty marketing. Since the second coming of The Natural Movement, coupled with the "Green" Movement — *Natural-Based* products and natural messaging product ingredients that boast of natural oils, nuts, or seeds, have become a recurring theme in the marketplace. On the opposite spectrum, *Science-Based* beauty products, manufactured fresh from labs are promoted by other brands.

Science-Based brands often use pseudoscientific terms like "cosmeceutical, therapeutic cosmetic, and Active treatment."

Innovative terms, yes? Innovative product efficacies — debatable. Whichever the approach, safeguarding credibility with clinical testing, helps advance the credibility and claim needle. But like Research & Development (R&D), clinical testing requires large budgets which many start-ups and established brands just don't have the funds for.

Innovation in Multi-Cultural categories during the 20th and 21st Centuries has been sluggish. This is surprising, based on the never-ending quest for beauty and continual search for "right" products.

MULTI-CULTURAL BEAUTY INNOVATION BENCHMARKS

- ➢ Straightening Comb – Invented by Egyptians, expanded upon by the French and then Annie Malone and the First Female Millionaires in the US, Madame C.J. Walker (initially heated with fire or used on a stove, later electric straightening comb) (Freeman Institute, 2016)

- ➢ Relaxer – Garret A. Morgan invented the relaxer, 1913, (Garrett Morgan, 2016).

- ➢ Permanent Ultra Wave— created by George E. Johnson in 1954. followed by women's chemical straighteners (Richard, 2015) (Essence.com, 2016).

- ➢ Lye Relaxer—Officially produced lye relaxer in 1971, by Proline

- ➢ No-Lye Relaxer – Introduced in 1981, with Gentle Treatment, the first no-lye relaxer. (Johnson Products , 2009)

- ➢ Jheri Curl - Comer Cottrel created the Jheri Curl, named for the stylist Jheri Redding. Cotrell created a dynasty with this invention, some report 1 out of 4 black people wore a Jheri Curl in the 1970's and 1980's, later adopted as a California Curl. (NPR.org, 2014)

- ➢ Edge Gel – A NEW Category, introduced by Hick's Edge Gel, in between an edge gel and pomade in consistency., in the 2000's. In recent years *colored edge gels* have emerged in the marketplace.

- ➢ Brazilian Keratin Treatment -Many suggest inventing the Brazilian straightening treatment, it came to the U.S around 2006.

The timeline above is an abridged innovation timeline within the Multi-Cultural haircare category. But overall, Multi-Cultural haircare innovation is more than flat. Tools have advanced the options— flat irons, tapered curling irons, hair dryers, including ceramic and tourmaline, but niche advancement is where the advancement lives and breathes.

DIGITAL BASED INNOVATION

The internet is responsible for new, progressive business models in the Beauty Industry. This includes pure retailing, product sampling—beauty boxes/auto replenishing business models and internet born brands with great stories.

SMART BRANDING

Curls Understood.com – A Blog, Beauty Box Subscription Box. One unique point of difference Curls Understood delivers is a consumer hair type evaluation that aligns your hair type with the best product efficacy match. There is also a consumer feedback as a measurement tool for brand partners.

INNOVATIVE BRANDS IN 2015

Prestige brands tend to have the most technological advancements, most likely attributed to the robust R&D budgets. Innovation = Investment. ($).
Noteworthy U.S. innovative brands:

1. Sephora IQ Color (2015)– This product scans the surface of our sin to give you a skin color, also provides matches for lip, foundation and concealer. With pantone (PMS)

colors. Brilliant!

2. Temptu-Air Skin Perfection Kit (2014) – A cordless airbrush system., leaves skin flawless and no-filter worthy.

3. Curl Clamp Straightener

4. Clarisonic Facial Cleansers (2006)

5. Huetiful Hair & Facial Steamer (2009)- Great for face and hair.

6. Pearl Compact Mirror with Phone Charger (2016) – The perfect duo.

7. Nails Inc. Spray on Nail Polish (2016) – Spray it on, when it dries the excess rinses off with a hand wash.

8. Living Proof Dry Shampoo (2005) – Makes your hair look and feel like it's been washed.

9. Cover FX Coverage Drops (2016) – One drop is sheer coverage; four drops create complete coverage. Added to water, serum or primer for a tinted moisturizer or foundation. And lasts a long time.

10. Sally Hansen Mani Match App (2016) – A Virtual Try-On App.

BEAUTY INFLUENCERS + BRAND INNOVATION

Innovation is another area where the Beauty Influencer shines naturally. Bloggers and Vloggers have their hearts and ears on the pulse of emerging trends. Multi-Cultural beauty habits influence mainstream trends. Understanding the types of products consumers want and need— particularly from the Naturalista community—is important and easy to capture and relay to beauty brands.

Beauty Influencers can lend support for beauty clients, as an authority for new brand discoveries of consumer interest and usage. Your blog/vlog is an excellent platform to showcase what's new with your brand. Couple that with social media or new social platforms like Periscope or Snapchat. Offering new social media platforms add value and differentiation, though consistency is critical so ensure the infrastructure is in place. Another offering to monetize through niche followers or audience.

THE FUTURE IN BEAUTY

The future of beauty belongs to those who "keep it fresh." Fresh in concept, usage and effectiveness. Products that meet needs and make life easier. New products that are robust rooted in Research and Development (R&D). But, R&D equals innovation, and innovation equals investment.

Is your new product a heavy R&D story? All-natural in messaging? Or, a science-based technology story? The truth is, in my experience at least 25 % or more of the innovation, is in the marketing and communication messaging used. So whether you're an entrepreneur with a start-up firm and a small budget, or an established beauty brand with multiple global R&D locations — smart communication and branding is key.

The method in which you present the product — as new, innovative in strategy, or with efficacy and usage strengths is critical. In addition to creative look and feel. The communication strategy can make or break your beauty brand.

AFTERWORD

Like all things in life, they change, they evolve. Beauty branding is a constant work in progress, ever changing alongside the NEW AGE OF BEAUTY. Digital, Technology, Social Media, the Multi-Culturally explosive population all require new navigation tools.

This book captures 15 years of experience, essential tactics and a proprietary new navigation tool The Beauty Breakthrough Theorem™.

The tactics and strategies in this book are not sealed in stone. They are ever-evolving. And with new seasons come new opportunities to navigate, implement, monetize, and measure.

My goal in writing this book is to share essential tactics and help make the beauty journey easier so that small brands can become big brands, and big brands can leave legacies. I want to help brands win. My audience for this book are three critical *Evolving Beauty Facets:*

The Entrepreneur

1. The independent beauty brand manufacturer, the start-up, the product beauty brand.
2. The Beauty Brand Influencers— Bloggers/Vloggers. Today they are brands of their own, the service beauty brand.

The Intraprenuers
3. Brand Executives managing the beauty brand from inside of the corporation

Evolving Beauty is about Beauty: Hair, Skin, Body.

This book is about the monetizing power that lives in a woman's perception of her identity and beauty. It's about the underappreciated power of women, their beauty dollars. The over-indexed beauty purchases by women of color, they still seek the "right" products with minute beauty advancements.

Innovation equals (=) R&D plus (+) Investment ($).

If you are one of these three types of *Evolving Beauties*, we want to hear from you. OR, if you are a beauty enthusiast — do tell. We want to hear your story. We're always interested in new tactics and perspectives. Share how *Evolving Beauty* impacted you. Thank you for engaging, friending and following: EvolvingBeauty.Info | @_EvolveBeauty

May you continue to Evolve!.– Love & Light!
~PT

EVOLVING BEAUTY AT A GLANCE

"Nothing is IMPOSSIBLE, the word itself means
I'M POSSIBLE!"
~Audrey Hepburn

SUMMARY

Below is a synopsis of each chapter and my predictions for the ever-evolving future of the Beauty Industry.

1 – THE BUSINESS OF BEAUTY IN A NEW AGE

- ➤ This book was meant to support
    - ○ Intreprenuers – Inside Corporate Brand Executives and
    - ○ Entrepreneurs – Start-Up Manufacturers,
    - ○ Product Brands and
    - ○ Beauty Influencers, Service Brands, to build brands independently and unite collectively.
- ➤ A new proprietary navigation tool, The Beauty Breakthrough™ was introduced (Taylor, Shine Beauty Culture Consultancy, 2016) that serves as a guide for big and small brands as they introduce new categories, determine partnerships, launch new products and create marketing and communication campaigns.
- ➤ The Multi-Cultural minority population will soon exceed the majority population in the U.S. – continuing to affect hair (texture) and skin (melanin/mixed layers/SPF infused) products.

- ➢ Diversity and Inclusion in the Beauty Industry is a requirement, not an option.
- ➢ The advanced technology within the Digital Age are key components of the future of the Business of Beauty.
- ➢ Integrated marketing plans with strong brand essence,
- ➢ culturally cued research, a niche audience and a robust competitive placement will become the most successful and leading edge in the business.
- ➢ The future of beauty products will be consumer-centric based on the variety in hair texture, skin / body color and melanin composition, as applicable.

2 – KNOW THY SELF

- ➢ There is a 3-Pronged Approach to building your brand with confidence that includes:
  - o Brand Essence
  - o Communication + Brand Story
  - o Rooted in Continual Growth + Innovation

3 - SOCIAL RESEARCH

- ➢ Research affords consumer insight and competitive marketplace analysis.
- ➢ Smart research connects insight to foresight.
- ➢ Cultural cues, purchase patterns (online and in-store) and lifestyle sensibilities are critical to effective, smart research.
- ➢ The opportunities in social research are abundant.
- ➢ Beauty Influencers are an excellent tool for peripheral research.

4 - BE YOUR OWN MASTER

> ➤ Work to own, understand and create a solid Brand Essence.
> ➤ Lead with the Cultural Cues from your tribe, your audience.
> ➤ Stand in your Brand Story, ever-evolving and is paramount to connecting with people, it distinguishes your brand from another commodity.
>> o There is a power in focusing on a *hero sku or skus.*
>> o Know your position within the competitive view.
>> o Brand imagery and creative extensions should reflect your Brand Essence.
>> o Develop proactive 360° campaigns versus reactive one-off projects.

5 - ISYNERGIZE + MEASURE

> ➤ Curated content aligned with your Brand Essence is King.
> ➤ Inbound Marketing works for big and small businesses.
> ➤ Seek the "right" social media platforms, it's not one size fits all.
> ➤ If you understand the online shopping behavior of your customer, you will win! Test, Analyze, Test, Analyze, Repeat.
> ➤ *Every* partnership and campaign should have Key Performance Indicators (KPIs)/ Success Metrics.

6 - SEEK BFF'S

> ➤ Seek win/win partnerships.
> ➤ Each partner should have something to contribute and something to gain.

o Corporate Social Responsibility Campaigns are under-utilized, and a smarter way of integrating charities will emerge.

7 - HAVE YOU BEEN CALLED?

➢ Entrepreneurship is a calling. It's not for everyone.
➢ Intelligence, common sense, conviction and passion, coupled with the "right" partnerships lead to profits.

8 - GET RETAIL READY!

➢ Using the BBT™ you can assess your national retail distribution readiness.
➢ Bricks & Clicks — Distribution is not one size fits all. Seek the best outlets, digital and brick and mortar. Bricks and Clicks.

9 - KEEP IT FRESH

➢ Innovation = Investment ($)
➢ Multi-Cultural innovation has been slow, but with the monetizing of new independent brands and strong consumer needs, I predict advancements will surface.
➢ Niche product offerings — customization by age, gender, ethnicity, format, texture and functionality will emerge with the best offerings.
➢ Multi-purpose products with strong efficacy will win.

OVERALL BEAUTY FORECAST

> *Power of Giving* - The optimist in me requires that I continue to see the beauty in all and continue to believe the world is good. And so, although the ultimate goal is to monetize opportunities, the beauty (no pun intended) of profits evolves, it's cyclical. Therefore, I am forecasting and hoping beauty brands will become actively involved with charities that support the causes important to the women their products are sold to.

> *Teamwork* – The days of the solopreneur are passe.' Although most entrepreneurs at least start out as solopreneurs. Working with teams or project collaborations are NEW AGE. Teamwork is required for smarter branding. Less time consuming work with greater life balance for what's important in your life. The emergence of communal workspaces across the country are a great example of the need for teamwork. Work communal spaces with flexibility. The freedom of being an entrepreneur, with the luxury to meet new business people, share ideas, get work done in a new space, meet with the project team to create and develop, but only as as needed.

> *Digital Leaders* - Brands that invest in product innovation, lead with smartphone integration, followed by digital video and advanced augmented reality for consumer beauty trial — will win.

REFERENCES

(2014, October 11). Retrieved from NPR.org: http://www.npr.org/sections/codeswitch/2014/10/11/354931324/comer-cottrell-creator-of-the-peoples-jheri-curl-dies-at-82

(2015). Retrieved from We Are Social: www.WeAreSocial.com

A.T. Kearney . (2014, May). Retrieved from A.T. Kearney : www.ATKearney.com

Advertising Age. (2015, December). *Top Bloggers*. Retrieved from www.adage.com: www.AdAge.com

Alexander, G., & Cunningham, M. (2005). *Queens*. New York, New York: Doubleday.

AT Kearney. (2014). *Beauty and the E-Commerce Beast*. Retrieved from AT Kearney: https://www.atkearney.com/documents/10192/5357723/Beauty+and+the+E-Commerce+Beast+-+2014+Edition.pdf/dcb3ec25-7274-484d-a9d2-a8f3fe488e4f

Dictionary.Reference.com. (n.d.). Retrieved from Dictionary.com: www.dictionary.reference.com

Dictionary.Reference.com. (n.d.). Retrieved from Dictionary.Reference.com

Discover Anthropology. (2015, July 1). *Discover Anthropology*. Retrieved from Discover Anthropology: http://www.discoveranthropology.org.uk/about-anthropology/what-is-anthropology/social-and-cultural-anthropology.html

Discover Anthropology. (2015, July 1). *Discover Anthropology*. Retrieved from Discovery Anthropology: http://www.discoveranthropology.org.uk/about-anthropology/what-is-anthropology/social-and-cultural-anthropology.html

Essence.com. (2016). *Black Hair Then, Now and Beyond*. Retrieved from Essence.om: http://photos.essence.com/galleries/black-hair-then-now-beyond?slide=11221

EuroMonitor Interantional. (2015). Retrieved from www.EuroMonitorInternational.com

EuroMonitor International. (2015, January 1). *Euromonitor*. Retrieved January 1, 2015, from Euromonitor: www.Euromonitor.com

ExpandedRamblings. (2016). *ExpandedRamblings.com*. Retrieved from ExpandedRamblings.com: http://expandedramblings.com/index.php/resource-how-many-people-use-the-top-social-media/

Freeman Institute. (2016). Retrieved from http://www.freemaninstitute.com/poro.htm

Garrett Morgan. (2016). Retrieved from http://www.biography.com/people/garrett-morgan-9414691

Guiness World Recordds. (1919, January 1). *Guiness World Records*. Retrieved January 1, 1919, from http://www.guinnessworldrecords.com/world-records/first-self-made-millionairess

Hana Ben-Shabat. (2015). *AT Kearney*. Retrieved from Global Retail E-Commerce Keeps on Clicking: https://www.atkearney.com/consumer-products-retail/e-commerce-index/full-report/-/asset_publisher/87xbENNHPZ3D/content/global-retail-e-commerce-keeps-on-clicking/10192

Harvard Business Review. (2009, March). *Ethnographi Research*. Retrieved from Harvard Business Review: https://hbr.org/2009/03/ethnographic-research-a-key-to-strategy/ar/1

HubSpot. (2015). Retrieved from State of Social Marketing: HubSpot.com

In Cosmetics. (2015). Retrieved from http://news.in-cosmetics.com/2015/10/dos-and-dont-for-digital-marketing-in-the-beauty-industry/

Investopedia. (n.d.). Retrieved from Investopedia: www.investopedia.com

Johnson Products . (2009, Dec 29). *Johnson Products You Tube Channel*. Retrieved from Johnson Products You Tube Channel: https://www.youtube.com/watch?v=V6msYzR6hvl

Kline Market Research . (2015). *Multi-Cultural Reporting*. Chicago: Kline Market Research.

Latson, J. (2014, December 23). *Time.com*. Retrieved from Time: http://time.com/3641122/sarah-breedlove-walker/

LinkedIn. (2016, January). *Social Media Active Users*. Retrieved from www.linkedin.co/pulse/social-media-active-users-216-spacecoastmarketing-inc

Lopez, A. (2013, August 7). *Forbes*. Retrieved from http://www.forbes.com/sites/adrianalopez/2013/08/07/passion-before-profit-following-your-passion-is-the-essential-entrepreneurial-trait/#2617de4b65a4

Market Research Association. (2015). *Zora Neale Hurston*. Retrieved from zoranealehurston.com: http://zoranealehurston.com/index.html

Matt Smith. (2015). Retrieved from http://onlineincometeacher.com/money/top-earning-blogs/

Merriam-Webster Dictionary . (2016). Retrieved from Merriam-Webster Dictionary : Merriam-Webster Dictionary.com

Nielson. (2015, January 1). Retrieved January 1, 2015, from Nielson: www.nielson.com

Opiah, A. (2014, January 24). *HuffingtonPost*. Retrieved January 18, 2016, from HuffingtonPost: http://www.huffingtonpost.com/antonia-opiah/the-changing-business-of-_b_4650819.html

QR Code Press. (2016, February). Retrieved from QRCodePress.com: http://www.qrcodepress.com/loreal-paris-develop-augmented-reality-beauty-application/8531844/ (

Research University of Florida. (2015, July 1). Retrieved from Research Publication University of Florida: www.research.ufl.edu/publications/explore/v07n1/zora.htm

Richard, C. A. (n.d.). Retrieved from EHow: http://www.ehow.com/about_5098213_history-hair-relaxers.html

Richard, C. A. (2015). Retrieved from http://www.ehow.com/about_5098213_history-hair-relaxers.html

Shareaholic. (2015, January). Retrieved from Shareaholic.com

SnapSurveys. (2016, March` 1). *SnapSurveys*. Retrieved from SnapSurveys: www.snapsurveys.com/qualitative-quantitative-research/

Society of Actuaries. (2005). The Stepping Stone. *Society of Actuaries* (18).

U.S. Census. (2014, October 4). *U.S. Census/Population*. Retrieved October 4, 2014, from U.S. Census: www.uscensus.com/population

University of Oregon. (2013). Retrieved from University of Oregon: http://blogs.uoregon.edu/j350dove/2013/06/10/summary

USA Today. (2015). Retrieved from USAToday.com: http://www.usatoday.com/story/tech/personal/2015/03/08/sephora-tech/24602349/

VentureBeat. (2015). Retrieved from VentureBeat: (http://venturebeat.com/2015/08/17/meerkat-says-users-are-more-engaged-than-ever-but-data-suggests-lackluster-growth/)

Wall Street Journal. (2015). Retrieved from www.blogs.wsj.com

Wong, J. (February, 5 2015). *Refinery 29*. (L. Perlstein, Producer) Retrieved from Refinery 29: http://www.refinery29.com/79682?collection=227

WWD. (2015, December 1). Beauty Inc. *Social Media Year of the Influencer 2015* , 27.

WWD. (2015, December 1). Corporate Social Responsibility of the Year. *Beauty Inc.* , 51.

WWD. (2015, December 1). Earned Media Valuation used a proprietary algorithm from Tribe Dynamics. *Beauty Inc.* , 27.

WWD. (2015, December 15). Social Media Year of the Influencer 2015. *Beauty Inc.* , 27.

ZoraNealeHurston. (2015, July 1). *ZoraNealeHurston*. Retrieved from ZoraNealeHurston: www.zoranealehurston

INDEX

161

ABOUT THE AUTHOR

"Culture, Beauty, Education, Diversity and People-I Cultivate Things!" ~PT

PhylenciaTaylor.com | EvolvingBeauty.Info |
ShineBeautyCulture.com
Connect @EvolvingBeauty.Info.

Phylencia "PT" Taylor is a Beauty Culturalist. She's inspired by beauty's ability to shape a woman's identity, image and her experience of the world. The monetizing power derived from a woman's perception of identity and beauty.

Taylor's passion for beauty runs deep, having worked with Fortune 500's for over a decade. Her beauty expertise is multi-faceted and well cultivated. She has worked in senior roles as Corporate Intrapreneur and a Beauty Entrepreneur: Chief Consultant and Founder of Shine Beauty Culture Consultancy (Est. 2007). A beauty framework of distinction, Taylor is set her insider advantage; working both sides of the business — Corporate and Agency. She is immersed in the Business of Beauty: a Beauty Culturalist, Content Curator, Inter-Cutlural Strategist and Beauty Consultant.

Taylor has a M.A. in Strategic Communication from American University, a BBA from Clark Atlanta University. She currently serves as an Adjunct Professor within the University System of

Georgia.

A native of upstate New York, she and her son live in a suburb of Atlanta, Ga.